Recycling

GLASS

RECYCLING

Jean F. Blashfield and Wallace B. Black

Education Consultant
Helen J. Challand, Ph.D.
Professor of Science Education, National-Louis University

Recycling Consultant
William Tarman-Ramcheck, Ph.D.
President, Associated Recyclers of Wisconsin
President, REC Systems of Wisconsin, Inc.

CHILDRENS PRESS ®
CHICAGO

A production of B&B Publishing, Inc.

Project Editor: Jean Blashfield Black
Designer: Elizabeth B. Graf
Computer Makeup: Dori Bechtel

Photo Researcher: Terri Willis
Cover Design: Margrit Fiddle
Artist: Valerie A. Valusek

Printed on Evergreen Gloss
50% recycled preconsumer waste
Binder's board made from 100% recycled material

Library of Congress Cataloging-in-Publication Data

Blashfield, Jean F.
    Recycling / by Jean F. Blashfield and Wallace B. Black.
        p. cm. -- (Saving planet earth)
    Includes index.
    Summary: Discusses the advantages of recycling and how we can help protect
the environment from further damage.
    ISBN 0-516-05502-X
    1. Recycling (Waste, etc.) -- Juvenile literature. 2. Refuse and refuse disposal --
Juvenile literature. 3. Environmental protection -- Citizen participation -- Juvenile
literature. [1. Recycling (Waste) 2. Refuse and refuse disposal. 3. Environmental
protection.] I. Black, Wallace B. II. Title. III. Series.
TD794.5.B63   1991
363.72'82--dc20   91-400
                                                                            CIP
                                                                            AC

Cover photo- © Imtek Imagineering/Masterfile

TABLE OF CONTENTS

Chapter 1

The Phantom
Garbage Barge

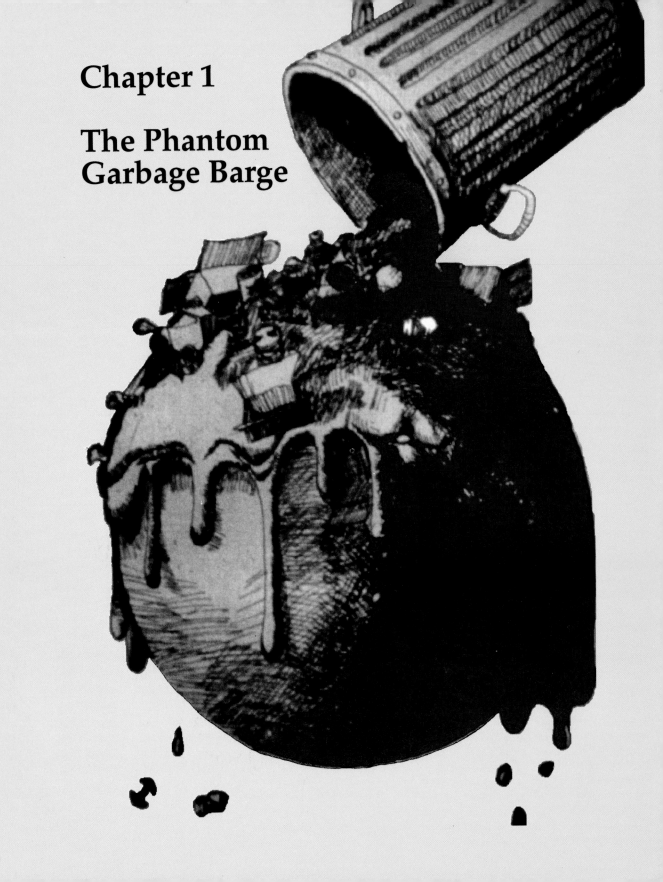

ON MARCH 22, 1987, the *Mobro*, a barge loaded with bales of trash from businesses on Long Island, New York, headed for an island near Morehead, North Carolina. Usually such garbage was put into a soil-covered hole called a *landfill* in the town of Islip, but that landfill was getting full. Businesses had been told that they would have to find other places to dump their waste.

A businessman from Alabama decided that he would help solve the problem by buying the trash. He planned to bury it and let it decompose under the soil. When air can't get to organic matter—food waste, paper, and other things that were once alive—it decomposes, giving off a gas called *methane*. The man hoped to collect methane and sell it as a fuel or as an ingredient in important chemicals.

But when the *Mobro*, carrying 3,100 tons of trash—about 160 truckloads—arrived in North Carolina, county officials would not allow it to unload. They were afraid that the cargo might contain harmful chemicals. Not wanting to take a chance on hurting their own environment, they sent the barge away.

One by one, the states of Alabama, Louisiana, Mississippi, Texas, and Florida also turned the barge away. The barge was then rejected in Mexico, Belize in Central America, and the Bahamas. By that time, people all over the world were reading about the *Mobro*—the "phantom barge" that was not allowed to land anywhere.

After traveling more than 6,000 miles in eight weeks, the garbage was taken back to New York where it lay at a Brooklyn dock for another three months, gathering more publicity and lots of sightseers. Brooklyn finally agreed to accept the garbage and burn it. The leftover ash—400 tons of it—was taken to the town of Islip, where it was put in the landfill that had rejected the waste in the first place.

At first, it seemed that the only result of the "phantom barge's" long journey would be its high cost. But the publicity led many people to wonder about the waste that we all create every day:

Where does it go after a truck picks it up at our curbs?

What happens to the trash after it has been collected?

If all that trash on the barge came from just one place, how much is in the state—the country—the continent—the whole world?

What will we do when there's nowhere left to dump trash?

If all those places rejected the trash because it might harm the environment, does that mean that our own trash is hurting our environment?

And, finally, what can we do to make sure that there's *less* trash to get rid of?

The man who bought the trash was hoping to *help* with the trash problem by using it to make methane gas. Anyone who used his garbage-made gas would not be using natural gas from the Earth, and part of an important natural resource would be saved.

And the garbage could have been used in other ways. The glass bottles, aluminum cans, plastic bottles, and newspapers in the trash could also have been used.

Using trash that would otherwise end up in a landfill is called *recycling.* As you'll discover in this book, many things can be recycled. Others can be reused. And, perhaps most

important, we can reduce the amount of trash we make in the first place!

When we reduce, reuse, and recycle, we save land space where the trash would have been dumped, and we protect the water and soil around dump sites. We also save energy if we don't have to make new products to replace things we throw away. We help keep the air from getting polluted by trash that would have been burned.

It has become clear in recent years that whatever one nation does on Earth affects other nations. We are one world—"Spaceship Earth"—and each one of us is responsible for taking care of it.

As the Mobro *waited at a Brooklyn dock to learn where its trash could go, environmentalists made sure that the world learned about recycling.*

9

Chapter 2

Humans,
The Garbage Makers

WE HAVE LEARNED A LOT about ancient people by studying what they threw away. Even the earliest people needed somewhere to throw the bones of the animals they ate and the waste from the grain they harvested.

Some people just dumped it on the ground inside their huts. When the ground got too messy or the bugs too numerous, they hauled some loose soil in and spread it over the garbage. After they did that a few times, they had trouble getting in their doors, so they built new huts. Later, people decided to keep the waste outside, so they carried it somewhere out of sight and dumped it in a pit. Year after year, they added more stuff to the pit. As people gathered together in towns, they just kept doing the same thing— dumping their garbage in pits.

Archeologists learn a lot about ancient people by digging down into these pits. They learn what the people ate, what tools they used, how they made clothing, what they played with—and how little they threw away.

In the last two hundred years, city governments took charge of getting rid of trash. But they just kept doing the

In nineteenth-century New York City, the streets became narrower as garbage mounted up. Insects and rats were everywhere.

11

When city workers go on strike, the trash piles up on the sidewalks as in the old days. Rodents, insects, and dogs disturb it. Soon there's no safe place to walk or play.

same thing—dumping everything into a convenient hole—and charging people for doing it. The trash created in a town is called *municipal waste.*

In the United States, Canada, and other countries with lots of land, people got used to throwing their trash in the town dump. If the dump caught on fire, as dumps often did, it didn't really matter. Usually the dump was outside of town where the people could neither see it nor smell it.

After a while, some towns saw that fire reduced the waste in the dump. They began to deliberately burn, or incinerate, the trash, even though it made unpleasant smoke.

FACT

You can walk one mile along the average highway in the United States and see about 1,457 pieces of litter—including paper, bottles, and fast-food containers that have been tossed out of car windows. If you crawled along at ground level, you would spot about four times as much. Most litter will never disappear unless it is picked up.

12

Messy garbage dumps, where trash lies out in the open, are being replaced by planned and managed landfills.

In regions with large populations but not much open land, such as Europe and Japan, the citizens had to start looking for other ways to dispose of their trash sooner than North Americans had to. But now it's time—in fact, it's past time—for all Americans and Canadians to start thinking about our habits.

The "Throwaway" Society

In the twentieth century, factories have become so efficient that products cost less and less to make. Most people no longer get things repaired or sell them to a "junk" man—who collected scrap many years ago. Most people in industrialized nations just throw away broken toys, worn-out appliances, and torn clothing.

The United States has sometimes been called the "throwaway" or "disposable" society because we throw so many things away and replace them with new ones.

Life has changed a lot in recent decades. The number of businesses using huge quantities of paper has increased. Selling through the mail has become important, but most people throw out the catalogs and mailing brochures they

People of the world have always viewed the oceans as convenient places to dump garbage. Recently, 14 billion pounds of trash have been added to the world's oceans each year. Much of it cannot decompose.

receive. Millions of babies are wearing billions of disposable diapers—great for the mothers but bulky for the landfills. TV dinners and fast foods have become the mainstay of many people's diet . . . and their excess packaging, like all packaging, ends up in the trash.

Today—and every day—in the United States, an average of 3.5 pounds of municipal trash is thrown away for each man, woman, and child—more trash per person than is created anywhere else on Earth.

Australians, who also live in a wide-open country, throw away almost as much. Scandinavians throw away less than half as much. The Japanese throw away slightly more than one-third as much, and in India, the average citizen discards barely a pound of trash each day.

You probably don't throw away 3.5 pounds of trash by yourself in any one day—unless you're cleaning out your closet. But the newspapers your family reads, cereal cartons, milk bottles, fast-food containers, computer printouts from your mother's or father's office, cans from your kitchen, grass and leaves from your yard, dirty oil from your car, even your old car itself when it can't be fixed any more—all those common things add up to more and more trash.

It would take 141 barges the size of the *Mobro* or more than 43,000 garbage trucks to carry away America's municipal waste for one day. And this does not even include the waste that enters our sewers or the heavy waste from factories and mines.

And the amount of garbage that Americans produce is growing at a rate two times faster than the population!

But what can we do with it? Where can we put it? How can we stop making so much of it?

Integrated Waste Management

Many years ago, naturalists and other people who love our outdoor world began to realize that we were harming our environment by dumping and burning our waste. The air was becoming polluted. Poisonous liquids were running out of decomposing garbage and polluting our water sources. They began to look for answers.

The naturalists know what our main answer must be: We must not throw away so much trash. We can *reduce* our trash by thinking twice about what we buy. We can *reuse* the things we buy until they are past repair, and then we can find other ways to use them so that the worn-out items can be remade—*recycled*—into new products. Products that can't be used over and over should be made only of material that can be recycled.

Composting is a fourth way of limiting waste. It is a method of using nature to recycle materials. Compost is a

Municipal trash collectors have always taken away most of what people put out, no matter what it was. Now we know there's no such place as "away." Many cities now collect part of the trash for recycling.

natural fertilizer made by the decomposition of food scraps and yard wastes.

These four ways of limiting what gets into the waste stream are often abbreviated as *3RC*. You'll learn a lot more about them in later chapters.

Reducing, reusing, recycling, and composting are the first four steps in *integrated waste management*. That means that a town is not limited to a single method of getting rid of waste. Instead, the government and the citizens are part of a total plan. You and your family can play a role in helping your town decide about the next two stages in integrated waste management.

Incineration. After citizens and businesses do as much 3RC as they can, there is waste left over. That's where controlled burning comes in. It's no longer a matter of just setting the town dump on fire. Instead, *waste-to-energy incineration* uses the heat from burning waste to make steam for generating electricity or heating buildings, thus saving fossil fuels. Unseparated trash has about half the fuel value of coal.

The world's largest incinerator that burns household trash for fuel is located near Paris, France. It burns 50 tons of waste every hour to run steam turbines that supply electricity to the area.

But this form of burning can give off many pollutants, especially carbon dioxide, which increases the "greenhouse effect," raising the temperature of our atmosphere. Sulfur and nitrous oxide from burning combine with oxygen in air to make acids. These chemicals are carried back to Earth in *acid rain*, which poisons the land and kills living things in ponds and lakes. Even the ashes removed from the fire

Integrated waste managers expect that 35 to 45 percent of our trash will soon be burned in waste-to-energy incinerators.

contain hazardous chemicals and metals. However, engineers are working on ways to trap those pollutants. The ash left after burning is usually taken to a landfill.

Waste-to-energy incineration sounds like a good solution to our waste problems because it actually produces something useful from the waste—energy—thus saving the Earth's coal or oil.

But remember—all the material that is burned has to be replaced by more natural resources. Oil has to be taken from the Earth to make more plastics. Trees have to be cut down to make more paper goods. And if the metals and glass are not removed from the trash, they have to be replaced, too.

Our Earth has a limited supply of natural resources. A few are *renewable*—they can be grown again, such as trees. But most are gone once they have been used. They are *nonrenewable*, except maybe over millions of years. Coal, oil, natural gas, and minerals that yield metals are all nonrenewable. So if we burn everything in our waste, we might as well have burned coal to make energy in the first place. Incineration of some things, however, does have a place in an integrated waste management program.

Landfills. Some trash cannot be burned because it gives off air pollutants that can't be trapped. This, along with ash from incineration, is taken to the *sanitary landfill*, the last stage in the integrated waste management system. Unfortunately, at present, most areas use landfills as the first step in eliminating trash rather than the last. But that habit cannot continue.

Landfills start out as pits specially prepared so that poisonous liquids cannot run out of the garbage and into the soil and water. They are usually dug in areas of heavy clay that prevents anything from seeping down through the soil. In addition, the pit may be completely lined with plastic.

Each day, waste collection trucks dump their trash into a landfill. Bulldozers then compact the material. At some landfills, a layer of dirt is spread over each layer of garbage—the same method the ancient people used in their houses.

A system of pipes collects the methane gas that is given

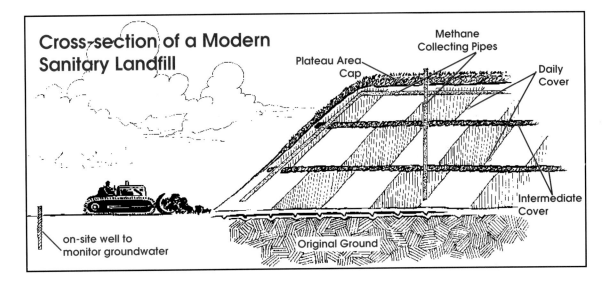

Cross-section of a Modern Sanitary Landfill

Methane Collecting Pipes

Plateau Area Cap

Daily Cover

Intermediate Cover

on-site well to monitor groundwater

Original Ground

off by the garbage as it decomposes. Methane is a large part of natural gas and it can be used in a variety of chemical products, or to heat houses—or even to run cars.

Wells are sunk deep into the earth around landfills to check that nothing toxic, or poisonous, is leaking into the groundwater. Finally, the landfill is capped by deep soil. When grass is planted, a landfill can become part of a park. Golf courses and playgrounds have been built on landfills.

Sanitary landfills sounded like a good idea when they were first used, but we've run out of space near cities. Trucks now carry city garbage to distant places, even other states, to dump it. Also, wells and streams near landfills are not as safe from water pollution as had been expected.

New York City's Fresh Kills Landfill oozes more than a million gallons of revolting, poisonous liquid into the ocean around Staten Island every day. As a benefit, the landfill produces enough methane each day to heat 50,000 homes. But the mountain of garbage will be as high as the law will allow by the year 2000. Then where will New York City send its trash?

At Fresh Kills Landfill on Staten Island, trucks line up all day to dump the trash collected in New York City. Fresh Kills is the largest landfill in the world.

FACT

For 5,000 years, the largest man-made structure on the Earth, by volume, was the Great Wall of China. In 1991, it will be overtaken by Fresh Kills Landfill on Staten Island, part of New York City. In use since 1948, the landfill covers 3,000 acres of swampy land and will soon be 500 feet high, making it the highest point of land on the East Coast.

As China modernizes, its people are producing 10 percent more trash each year! It is working hard to become a large industrial nation. Its industrial waste alone would require an annual landfill occupying 13,000 acres and polluting an additional 7,000 acres of farmland. But with more than a billion people, the Chinese can't use land for landfills. The people have to recycle everything possible.

In Egypt, trash collection and sorting has traditionally been the task of a caste of people called the *zabbaleens*, who are born into the job and do it all their lives. But the number of zabbaleens is dwindling, and municipal collection of waste is on the rise. Egypt is now building landfills in the desert, far from the cities.

Obviously, landfills are useful, but they should be used only for that small portion of waste that can't be handled in any other way.

Take a Look Back

An Earth Experience

Have a talk with your grandparents and, if possible, your great grandparents, about the "good old days." What were kitchens and stores like during the first part of this century? Here are some of the stories they might tell:

We had big gardens and planted fruit trees. Why waste the ground to grow a lawn when it could help feed us?

We canned many different foods when they were in season and reused the same jars year after year.

We made our own bread, desserts, jams, pickles, butter, candy, and beverages.

We didn't eat "junk food" because there wasn't any.

The country store had fresh foods and basic supplies such as flour and beans in barrels, bins, and cloth sacks. We took purchases home in baskets that we brought to the store or in rolled-up newspapers.

What is it like today? Take a good look in your kitchen cabinets and at the shelves in the grocery store. What kind of packages do things come in? What materials are thrown away in relation to the useful part?

Separate some food from its packaging. Weigh each one separately. What can you conclude?

How can you change the way your family shops or prepares food in order to cut down on the amount of trash produced in your home?

What's in Our Trash?

Until recently, nobody really thought about what we threw away. More important, very few people questioned whether we should be throwing it away at all. Oh, some scientists predicted that someday we would run out of certain minerals if we weren't careful, but that "someday" seemed far in the future.

But never before have there been so many people on the planet. Also, never before have there been so many uses for Earth's natural resources. Never before have there been so many people buying so many things and then throwing them away when they were through with them.

But there's no such place as "away." Garbage doesn't magically disappear.

At first it seemed that sanitary landfills would solve all our garbage problems. About 80 percent of all trash in the United States is dumped in landfills where, people assumed, garbage decomposed. They were wrong.

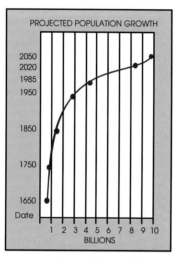

Not until about 1840 were there a billion people on Earth. Population scientists think we'll reach 7 billion by the year 2000.

"Garbologist" at Work. Their views began to change when archeologist William Rathje of the University of Arizona had his students dig into landfills to see what they could discover about people by the trash they discarded. The students put on rubber gloves and then sorted, cataloged, and analyzed eight tons of trash from several landfills around the western half of the United States. That started the

What We Throw Away

40%

17%

10%

9%

9%

7%

6%

2%

One year's waste for a
typical North American family

Garbage Project, which studies landfills all over the country.

What the students found, and what Rathje, who now calls himself a "garbologist," has confirmed since then, is not what people expected.

They thought, for example, that fast-food containers would be a big item in landfills because people talked so much about them being a problem. Yet Rathje found that they amounted to only about one-tenth of 1 percent of the waste. People were also sure that disposable diapers were a problem. Yet Rathje found that less than 1 percent was diapers. However, people were right about plastics being a big space user. They turned out to be only 7 percent by weight but closer to 15 percent by volume, and that percentage keeps increasing. Currently, plastic takes up about 20 percent of the space in landfills.

However, the biggest item Rathje found in the landfills was paper—huge quantities of Sunday newspapers and telephone books. And much of it hadn't even begun to decompose—even though some had been buried as long as forty years. Newspapers were still readable right down to the smallest type, and brown paper bags, which environment-conscious people had been choosing over plastic bags, had not degraded any better than plastic bags, which took up less room in the landfills.

Rathje thinks that North Americans today are not actually producing more garbage than our ancestors did a hundred years ago, but that ours is a different kind of garbage. One hundred years ago, most municipal waste consisted of heavy ash from coal-burning furnaces and dead horses. Today it's paper and grass clippings. And, of course, we have a lot more people.

Investigators for the Garbage Project use a big auger to dig 90 feet down into old landfills (above). The materials brought up are weighed and classified in the field (right). Finally, they are sorted and recorded (below).

"Garbologists" found hot dogs that were completely undecomposed after ten years in a landfill (center right). After 20 years, plastic film (bottom right) was found to be slimy but still whole.

Landfills act almost like museums in preserving evidence of our wastefulness. We're learning that our waste problem is not going to be solved with one grand gesture, such as getting rid of disposable diapers or outlawing the use of plastics. Things will change only if each of us does everything possible to keep waste out of the landfills.

An Earth Experience

If Your Family Hasn't Been Recycling . . .

Once a day, collect all the trash from the wastebaskets in your home. Weigh the items on your bathroom scale.

Sort out all the items that could be recycled or reused—glass, newspapers, cardboard, aluminum cans, steel, most plastics, nonmeat food scraps, and clothing. Now weigh only the materials that can't easily be recycled, such as meat, items made of mixed plastics, and coated papers.

Do the same thing daily for a week or two. Keep track of each category of waste—recyclable and nonrecyclable—that your family discarded.

What percentage of the solid wastes thrown away could have been recycled? Were there some items that might have been repaired if you had the skill to do it? Were there some items that could not be recycled at all? Study those items, and think about how your family uses them. Is there any way that you can cut down on those items?

Think about what you learned by studying your own trash. If your family has not yet begun to recycle trash, what you learned may encourage you to do so on a regular basis. Use your results to educate all your family members on the need to reuse and recycle.

Trash, A Natural Resource

If you think about each of the items you throw away, you may realize that you're not throwing away some vague thing called "garbage." It's not just a can, it's aluminum or steel. It's not just a test paper from school, it's fiber from trees. It's not just a broken plastic toy, it's petroleum. When our trash is taken to a landfill, we are throwing away resources from the Earth. That's the only place we get materials to make products. Even food ultimately comes from nutrients in the sea or land.

What does that tell you? It should tell you that someday we're going to run out of the natural resources we need if we keep throwing away our trash. We must start thinking of trash as a natural resource, too. The only way to do that is to keep waste products out of the landfills or incinerators where they cannot be used again.

It's wonderful that we can help the Earth in three different, important ways by doing just one thing. We can save our land from being taken over by landfills. We can keep pollution out of our air and water. We can save natural resources for the future.

All by reducing, reusing, and recycling our trash.

Chapter 3

Reduce, Reuse, Recycle

NOT EVERYTHING WE BUY can be recycled yet, so a person who wants to help save the Earth has to shop in a special, Earth-conscious way. As a *consumer*—a person who buys and uses up products—you must take a good look at things you consider buying. Think twice, and then think again, before you buy things that can't be recycled.

Remember the three Rs of 3RC. *Reduce* the waste you make. *Reuse* those items you can. Then, *recycle* everything possible.

The First R—Reduce

Making the right choices before you buy is the first R—*reduce* trash you make by not buying products that waste our resources. Sometimes this is called *precycling*.

The most important way to precycle is to think twice before buying any item. If a TV commercial for a game catches your attention, try to learn more about it before you buy. Make sure it's a game you'll want to play many times, or one you can pass on to others. An item of clothing may be right in style now, but will you still want it two months from now?

When you're in a store and looking at something you think you'd like to buy, ask yourself: Where will this product be in a week, a year, ten years?

Disposables. Reducing waste really consists of two parts, and both of them involve making smart choices before you buy. First, avoid buying throwaway items. Such products as disposable razors, ballpoint pens, paper plates, and cameras are available in versions that don't get thrown away after

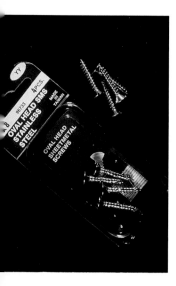

A shopper who thinks about the environment will choose to count out four screws from a bin of screws instead of buying screws in excess packaging that will just get thrown away, especially "bubble" packs that cannot be recycled.

one or a few uses. Those versions may cost a bit more in the first place, but they last, and last, and last.

A man who uses disposable razors may toss out between 3,000 and 4,000 of them during his life. Suppose that 100 million men in the United States and Canada are using disposable razors—that's an awful lot of mixed plastic and steel that can't be recycled.

Plastic is intended to be strong and durable. Buy only those plastic products that you'll use for a long, long time, such as eyeglasses, compact disks, flower pots, or dishes that you intend to wash. If the product you are considering buying is for short-term use, such as a disposable pen, a juice box, or a hamburger box, don't buy it.

With our Earth in trouble, it's appalling that an item can sit on a store shelf for a few days at most, be used once, and then sit in a landfill for several hundred years!

Wasteful Packaging. You can also reduce waste by choosing products that do not use excess packaging. A large part of the trash we throw away consists of packaging—drink containers, food cartons, plastic-covered display cases, foil trays, and the like.

A great deal of packaging consists of combinations of materials that can't be recycled. So-called "bubble" packs,

FACT

Out of every $10 we spend buying things, $1, or 10 percent, goes for packaging that we throw away. But that packaging represents about 65 percent of our household trash.

A package containing a frozen microwavable dinner includes the plate, the foil cover for heating it in a regular oven, a plastic cover for heating it in the microwave, and the wax-coated outer box. That's four pieces of trash—just to let you fix a dinner quickly. The meat and vegetables in the serving on the left were bought in bulk, reducing trash.

for example, consist of a cardboard backing with a plastic bubble protecting and showing the product. These are often used to hold perhaps a dozen screws or one makeup brush or a miniature car. Such packaging exists primarily to keep people from stealing small items from stores.

When you have a choice, buy the bare, unpackaged item. Pick tomatoes from a pile of tomatoes instead of from a pile of plastic-wrapped packages. Fresh fruits and vegetables do not need to be placed on a Styrofoam plate wrapped in plastic film. Choose a baseball from a case instead of from a row of bubble packs.

Another way to reduce packaging is to buy in bulk. If you use a lot of detergent or macaroni, for example, buy the bigger box. There's less packaging per washing or serving when you buy the bigger box. Buy cookies that come in bulk sacks rather than in plastic-lined foil bags that hold a few cookies in little plastic racks. You'll save money as well as reduce waste.

If you buy just one item, carry it out of the store instead of having it put in a bag. When you are grocery shopping, take your own reusable string bag or plastic sack with you. Some stores are now taking a few cents off the cost of your purchases if you bring your own bag.

A Precycle How-To

The city of Berkeley, California, has suggested the following summary of ways to precycle or reduce waste:

1. Select products carefully. Consider the environmental impact of every purchase you make.

2. Be picky about packaging. Pick paper, not mixed packaging. Look for the recycling symbol. It means that the package is made from recycled material or can be recycled.

3. Fight against overpackaging. Don't buy those products that come in excess packaging. Choose the alternative item that doesn't waste so much material.

4. Avoid polystyrene foam whenever possible. If you're eating in a fast-food restaurant, ask to get your food in paper instead of in a Styrofoam box.

5. Avoid disposable items.

6. Buy in bulk. More and more grocery stores are carrying dried and other items in bulk so that you can purchase several pounds at once instead of having to buy lots of little, more expensive packages.

7. Let store managers know what you think about the packaging you see or ask them to get environmentally safe items that you don't see.

The Second R—ReUse

When you're choosing a product to buy, think about how long you will use it. Make sure that you can *re*use it. Students at the University of Wisconsin in Madison carry red plastic coffee mugs instead of getting a disposable Styrofoam cup every time they purchase coffee, tea, or hot chocolate at the Student Union. They are keeping those difficult-to-recycle cups out of the waste stream.

The city of Portland, Oregon, has outlawed the use of polystyrene foam by restaurants and food vendors. One inspector, often called "Styro-Cop," visits restaurants throughout the city looking for violations of the law. He says, "To use plastic to drink 8 ounces of coffee for 2 minutes and throw it away where it will take up space forever is absurd."

Some Ways to Reuse Things. Think of new ways to use products instead of throwing them away.

Railroad ties are excellent for blocking in raised beds for strawberries, melons, or tomatoes. They can also be used to box in a compost pile.

Clothing and other items that you can't reuse can be passed along to someone else in a garage sale to keep them out of the waste stream.

33

Completely new and different uses can sometimes be found for certain items. For example, tires are often sunk into ocean water to serve as the base for reef formation (above). Seeds can be planted in polystyrene egg cartons and aluminum pie dishes (right).

Newspaper pages, especially the comics, make excellent gift wrapping. Always save and reuse ribbons and bows from year to year.

Use crumpled newspapers for packing breakables rather than Styrofoam "peanuts," which take hundreds of years to disintegrate.

Repairing is another R that keeps valuable materials out of the waste stream. Learn how to mend, replace a zipper, and develop other skills that make clothes last longer. Take unwanted clothing to resale shops or to centers for the needy, such as Goodwill Industries, where they are repaired by handicapped people, or to the Salvation Army.

The Third R—Recycle

Recycling is often called *resource recovery* because it is not just keeping things out of the waste stream by using them, it is actually recovering and reusing natural resources. Trash is a resource and trash cans are "mines above ground."

In the 1960s and 1970s, many individuals and groups

collected aluminum cans and took them to a *buy-back center* where they were paid a small fee.

Later, people who were concerned about waste began to take the material they accumulated to a *drop-off site* where the materials were bundled up and transported to a recyclables dealer. Unfortunately, many such drop-off sites disappear because of lack of volunteers, especially when the price paid for recyclables goes down.

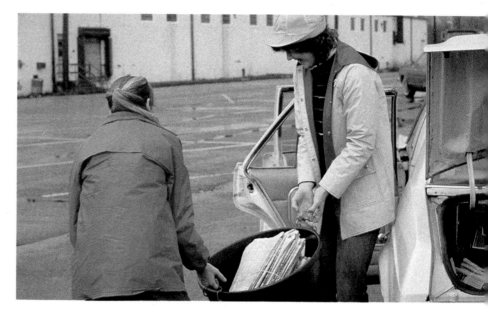

Homeowners can bring recyclables to a convenient drop-off center, where they are collected for recycling.

Some towns began to recycle officially in the late 1970s. This often happened when town officials realized that their landfill was becoming too full or when it was costing too much to send their trash elsewhere.

The simplest way for a town to recycle is to have the residents separate certain items when they put out their trash. This is called *curbside recycling*, although it is actually

The city of Seattle, Washington, has curbside recycling, meaning that residents separate their trash into several different recyclables for collection.

only one stage in the whole process of recycling. It is also called *source separation* because the different kinds of materials are separated by the people who throw them away. In 1986, the state of Rhode Island became the first state to require residents to separate their trash.

To curbside recycle, bundle newspapers together. Keep aluminum cans separate from your other waste. If your town recycles steel, keep the steel cans (after rinsing them out and flattening them) in another container. Keep plastic items in another container, and glass in another. If you can, remove the paper labels from both steel and glass containers. Finally, collect all remaining trash in a separate bag or trash can.

Towns that do curbside recycling may collect special items on special days. If they have trucks designed for recycling, they pick up all the containers on the regular day and dump them into separate compartments in the trucks.

It's not so easy to curbside recycle if you live in an apartment building. Find out what your building does with its trash and how you can help make sure that the waste actually gets recycled.

Sometimes toxic materials are picked up for special handling. These might include used motor oil, old cans of paint, batteries, or even aerosol cans.

The recycling symbol shown throughout this book has three curved arrows making a circle, symbolizing the three parts of the recycling process: *collection* of the waste materials, *production* of new products, and *purchase* of the new product by a new person. You'll learn more about these three activities in the following three chapters.

When you see the three-part symbol, however, you should also think of the three Rs that will help limit the waste that is endangering our planet if we don't act now. *Reduce—reuse—recycle.*

With imagination and concern for the environment, people can reuse, repair, or recycle items that might otherwise be hauled away to a landfill.

Chapter 4

Nature,
The Original Recycler

RECYCLING IS A SIMPLE IDEA. It means doing whatever is necessary to reuse an object. It can be as easy as washing a glass instead of throwing a plastic or paper cup away and using a new one. It can require a little planning, such as selling a coat at a garage sale. When someone else uses it, you've recycled it.

Recycling can also be very complex, as when a manufacturer finds a way to reuse or sell waste material left over from the manufacturing process instead of discarding it.

In nature, very little is ever discarded. Nature has wonderful ways of recycling so that the environment is continually freshened. Water, the organic nutrients in the soil, and some elements such as carbon and nitrogen are among the items that nature recycles.

Elements in Nature

When the solar system was formed out of spinning elements in the galaxy, the Earth acquired all the materials that it would ever have. Since then, these materials have been recycled and recycled for more than four billion years. Most of these recycled elements involve living creatures in some way.

The Carbon Cycle. Carbon, the basic element of life, is moved through nature in a continuous flow. As the compound carbon dioxide (CO_2), it is present in the air and taken in by plants. During the process of *photosynthesis*, the energy in sunlight, with the help of chlorophyll, converts the CO_2 and water to sugar and oxygen. The oxygen is released back into the air, from which animals breathe it in. Perhaps

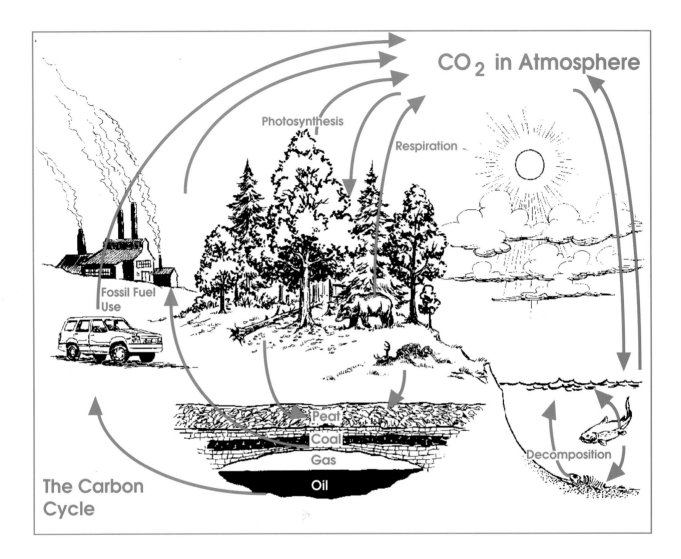

The Carbon Cycle

CO$_2$ in Atmosphere

Photosynthesis

Respiration

Fossil Fuel Use

Peat
Coal
Gas
Oil

Decomposition

the plants are eaten by animals. Some of the carbon becomes part of the animals' bodies as they grow. Some is given off during respiration when both animals and plants use oxygen and give off carbon dioxide. That CO$_2$ is then available in the atmosphere again for plants to take in.

However, much of the carbon remains as part of living organisms. When they die and fall to the ground, their cells decay through the action of bacteria and fungi. That action releases carbon into the soil where it is available for plants to use again. Or the animal body might fall into water, where it sinks to the bottom and decomposes. Hard parts might turn into rock, trapping the carbon.

Millions of years ago, during the Carboniferous Period, the Earth was covered with massive plants and living things swarmed in ancient seas. When they died, some of these plants and animal bodies gradually changed into petroleum and coal. Those fossil fuels now lie deep inside the Earth where they tie up a great deal of Earth's carbon. Modern people mine petroleum and coal from the Earth and burn it in factories and automobile engines, releasing more carbon dioxide into the atmosphere than the plants can handle.

The presence of fungi indicates that the tree is probably dead. The fungi decompose the wood, releasing basic nutrients for other plants to use.

Other Elements. Nitrogen, sulfur, and phosphorus are recycled in similar processes. Nitrogen gas, N_2, makes up about 78 percent of the atmosphere. However, living things

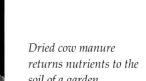

Dried cow manure returns nutrients to the soil of a garden.

41

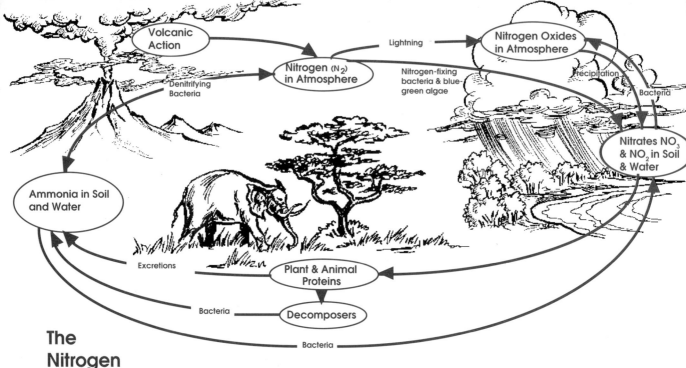

The Nitrogen Cycle

cannot use it directly. It has to be "fixed" for organic use. That means that it has to be turned into compounds called *nitrites* and *nitrates* that organisms can use. Lightning does some "nitrogen fixing," but most is done by algae in the oceans and bacteria on land. Plants and animals take the nitrogen-fixed compounds into their bodies, and release them only when they die and decay.

Unfortunately, we put a lot of excess nitrogen into the atmosphere by burning wood and fossil fuels. The nitrogen then combines with water vapor in the air to form nitric acid, part of the acid rain that is destroying forests and lakes.

Sulfur moves through our world in similar fashion. It has to be in the form of *sulfates* for living things to use. But some human activities put sulfur dioxide back into the air where it forms sulfuric acid, also part of acid rain.

Phosphorus, an even more important element, is included in DNA, the basic molecule of life. It is used by organisms in the form of *phosphates*. Phosphorus enters the environment mainly through the erosion of rocks or by *leaching,* the movement of water through soil that contains phosphorus. Those compounds are also recycled through animal manure entering soil.

In primitive countries and rural areas everywhere, pigs are handy recyclers. People feed them food scraps. The pigs, in turn, provide manure for fertilizing crops and are butchered for meat, while food scraps are fed to the next generation of baby piglets. You may not be able to keep pigs, but you can use some of nature's ways of recycling.

Composting

For many years, people piled up grass clippings and dried leaves, and then burned the pile. The smell of burning autumn leaves became a familiar odor in October. But burning gives off polluting carbon dioxide. The wonderful smell disappears very quickly, the excess CO_2 does not.

Recently, in most towns and cities, homeowners have been required to put their garden waste in plastic bags, which are picked up by trash collectors. Yard and food waste has been taking up more than one-fourth of the space in landfills. These wastes can't be incinerated because of the moisture in them.

Many cities pick up autumn leaves from gutters with a special truck (left). The leaves need to be composted because even organic matter may not decompose in a landfill. This grass (below) was buried in a landfill for 20 years.

But these materials are not really waste. They contain ready-to-use nutrients from nature's recycling system. There are other things we can do.

First, we can cut grass in a way that minimizes yard waste. If you set the lawn mower blade at its lowest level, you then have to rake up the long clippings. You can save considerable labor by letting the grass grow to between 3 and 5 inches long and trimming only the top third once a week, letting the clippings lie where they fall. They will sink back into the earth, returning nutrients, especially nitrogen, to the soil. Even a well-fed lawn will use at least 25 percent less fertilizer if clippings are used to feed it.

Composting is a second way of recycling organic nutrients. Compost is a mixture of decaying organic matter that can be used as fertilizer. In the past, country people often just threw their garbage out into the fields and let it decompose naturally. The process can be speeded up in a compost pile or heap.

Most food scraps except meat and fats can be chopped up and put in a compost heap. They should be added to the heap each day until it is large enough to start processing.

Conditions for Organic Decay

You can discover for yourself what conditions are most helpful in encouraging the breakdown of organic matter into its nutrients.

Dig up a bucket of good loam or topsoil from a wooded site or natural grassland—it will be richer in nutrients and decomposers than the "dirt" in your own backyard. Put this soil into five clay pots. Heat one pot filled with soil in a 300° F. oven for one-half hour. Label this pot #1.

Cut five slices of raw apple or potato. Measure the slices to be sure they are the same size and thickness and record these figures. Bury one slice in the center of each pot. Pots #1 and #2 can be left on your kitchen counter. Put pot #3 in a refrigerator. Place #4 where it will receive full sun all day. Place #5 where it will receive equal sun and shade during the daylight hours.

Water each pot except #2 each week. Otherwise, do not disturb your experimental setup for four weeks.

At the end of that time, dump the contents of each pot out onto newspaper. Carefully study each slice of potato or apple. Record what you observe about its color, size, and results of any break-down. What do you conclude about the conditions that promote the decomposition of organic materials in nature?

All living things contain both carbon and nitrogen, but in different combinations. Wood, for example, has at least 500 times more carbon than nitrogen. Grass clippings contain only about 20 times more carbon than nitrogen. The best mixture for making a good compost heap contains material that averages out at about 30 times more carbon than nitrogen. To get that balance, mix food scraps (even coffee grounds, fruit rinds, and eggshells) with yard waste (grass, leaves, and wood chips). Meat scraps should not be put into a compost heap because they attract rodents and may cause the compost to smell.

Microbes in the soil begin the process of decomposition. Fungi join in, then centipedes and millipedes enter the picture. Finally, earthworms break up, loosen, and aerate the mixture. The final product is a nutrient-rich soil called *humus*. Humus added to regular garden soil loosens it so that oxygen can reach plant roots. It helps hold water, and it provides extra nutrients. Mixed with the barren soil stripped from surface mines or spread on top of landfills, composted humus can make green things grow.

A well-balanced compost pile will make usable humus (organic soil) in about two or three months in warm weather. While the process of decay is going on in a compost heap, a great deal of heat is produced. That heat kills some weed seeds and disease-carrying organisms.

Composting keeps garden waste out of the landfills. It also eliminates organic matter that might prevent your regular trash from being recycled. If you normally use a garbage disposal, composting saves water and keeps garbage out of the sewage system. And it returns to the Earth the nutrients that came from it originally.

A garden compost heap (above) *is a convenient, environmentally sound way to reuse food and garden wastes. A New York City recycling firm reduces tons of organic wastes to tiny pellets of compost fertilizer* (right) *in less than 60 hours.*

Municipal Composting. Many towns and cities are now providing municipal compost heaps for people who do not want to compost in their own backyard, and for restaurants or food packagers that produce a great deal of organic waste. Towns sometimes add organic material such as paper or chopped-up natural textiles to the mix.

Large composting establishments make long piles of raw material, called *windrows.* Machines go down the rows, turning the material. When it has decomposed, the decayed material is sifted through a screen that catches any large pieces of garbage that didn't decay, or bits of glass and plastic that were not found in the original sorting.

It sounds as if a compost heap or windrows might be unpleasant to be near. But any odor disappears when the material is turned. Insects will probably not be interested. Rodents and pets are usually drawn only to garbage containing meat, which should be omitted.

Making Your Own Compost

Locate a spot in your yard that has equal amounts of sunlight and shade. Check to see if your town has laws that dictate the size of a compost pile and its distance from your neighbor's property.

Dig a pit two feet wide and six feet long. It should be about two feet deep to encourage soil creatures to enter it. Erect a wall around the pit. Old railway ties stacked on top of each other make an attractive box—and you are recycling the ties! If you can't find railway ties, use scrap lumber or a wire fence. Snow fences work well, and now they are often made of recycled plastic.

An Earth Experience

The wall should be just high enough to reach over comfortably so that you can turn the rotting material once a week and push a stick down into the pile at various places. This lets in air, which speeds up the decomposition.

You are now ready to add the compost material. Start with a layer of branches so that air can enter the mixture from underneath. Then add leaves, grass clippings, weeds, fireplace ashes, spoiled fruits and vegetables, and coffee grounds. If you chop up leaves and twigs, they will decompose more quickly.

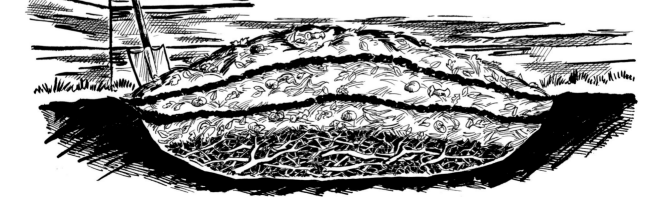

You may want to alternate layers of organic waste with thin layers of soil to introduce microbes into the mix more rapidly. Spray the pile with water to make it moist but not soggy. If a heavy rainfall is expected, you will need to cover the pit with plywood or plastic to keep it from getting too wet. If it accidentally gets water-soaked, add more dry material.

It takes several weeks for decomposition to begin.

The temperature rises inside the heap so, even over a cold winter, it does not freeze. If your mixture does not get hot in the middle, it probably needs more nitrogen-rich material. Add some manure or bloodmeal from a garden shop.

After several months, the mixture stops heating up. By that time, the material will have shrunk to about one-fifth of its original volume and disintegrated into fine pieces. It will be crumbly and dark-brown in color, and it will have a deep earthy smell like the heart of a forest.

This homemade humus supplies the calcium, phosphorus, lime, nitrogen, and

potassium needed for plant growth. You are recycling the elements back into the soil where they will once again be available for living things to use.

Recycling Water

As with organic nutrients, nature generally finds a way to keep water recycled, provided that humans do not interfere with the natural processes.

There is just about the same amount of water on and in the Earth now as there was when water appeared on the developing planet. Water is used and reused, but rarely is it actually ever *used up.* Instead, it changes from a liquid into a gas or a solid for a while or it is trapped—in glaciers, for example.

Nature recycles and cleans water through a cycle of *evaporation*—when the water changes to a gas—and *condensation*—when it changes back into a liquid. You have seen the principle, but just to remind yourself, you might try the following:

An Earth Experience

Discovering the Water Cycle

Heat a kettle of water on the stove. When it starts to boil, you will see steam rising from the spout. Actually, the visible steam consists of tiny water droplets. The water vapor being given off is invisible.

The burner represents the energy from the sun causing the liquid to evaporate. The air above the rising steam becomes concentrated with water vapor.

Now, using kitchen mitts, hold the flat bottom of a metal cake pan several inches above the steam coming from the spout. The pan represents the atmosphere. As the water vapor hits the cool surface, it condenses on the bottom of the pan and drops begin to form. They will fall as raindrops fall on Earth.

On the Earth, rain falls. It runs off the land into the rivers and lakes, from which it evaporates in the sunshine. In the cool atmosphere, the water vapor condenses. Clouds form, rain falls, and the cycle continues.

People interrupt Earth's normal water cycle in order to use the water for a while. Water might be run into the Earth for irrigation of agricultural crops. It might be taken from the lakes, purified, and piped into our homes. There we drink it, bathe in it, and use it to flush toilets or wash dishes. It might be used by a factory to cool machinery or to wash manufactured parts.

Recycling our Water Supply. A few people living by a river can return dirty water to the river, which will cleanse itself. But a city of thousands of people must clean the water

Factories often pour tons of pollutants into rivers. This is the Wisconsin River being polluted by a paper mill.

before returning it to nature. Dirty water leaves our homes through pipes that lead into a *sewage system.*

In a sewage system, the solid human waste (along with food and other items washed into the water) is allowed to settle out of the water, making a heavy, thick material called *sludge.* Sludge can be dried and burned or landfilled. However, human waste, like cow manure, is filled with nitrogen and phosphorus that can be returned to the soil.

In many countries of the world, human waste, often called *night soil,* is still collected in carts and taken to farmland where it is worked into the soil. However, this night soil often contains parasitic worms and harmful microbes, and it should be heat-treated before being used.

In many cities, sludge is put on farmland as fertilizer. First, however, it is allowed to be broken down by bacteria. The finished product has no odor or threat of disease. Some other cities send their sludge to municipal compost piles, where it enriches the humus made from garden waste.

After the solids have been removed from waste water, the water itself is cleaned, although many chemicals that people put down drains cannot be removed. Then it is allowed to flow back into the river, lake, or stream from which it came. Perhaps, as the used and recycled water flows on, it will be drawn from the river again and used once more.

About 30 percent of American houses dispose of waste water through *septic systems.* A septic system has a collecting tank where solid matter settles. Then pipes send the water out into an underground field where it slowly trickles through the soil back down into the water table. The collecting tank is pumped out periodically by a special truck that takes the solid material to a municipal sewage system.

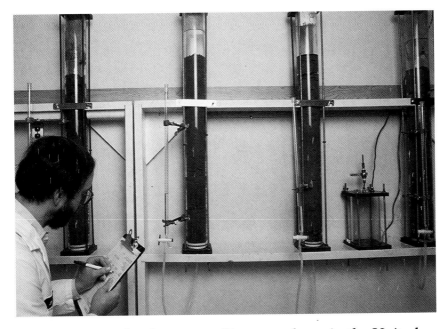

Unfortunately, there are still many places in the United States and around the globe where filthy water is fed directly back into rivers and streams or the ocean. With increases in population and the number of ways we use water, some lakes, rivers, and streams have become so polluted that all life in them has died. Salt from roads, weedkillers from fields, phosphates from detergents, chemicals that we dump down our drains, and discharge from factories affect our water supply. Together they can kill the life and usefulness of a river or lake.

A "dead" water source can sometimes be cleaned up and brought back to life with the combined effort of all the people and industries around it. This happened to Lake Erie in the United States, the River Thames in England, and other bodies of water in areas where people cared enough about their environment to take action.

Chapter 5

Paper, The Monster
in the Landfill

THE "GARBOLOGISTS" WHO ANALYZE what we throw away report that paper makes up a whopping 40 percent of all our waste. Yet paper is the easiest material to recycle!

Think about the kinds of paper you throw away each day—cereal boxes, newspapers, old school papers, cartons, and the like. Of the 3.5 pounds of waste you get rid of each day, almost a pound and a half is paper. Of all the waste reaching a landfill, 40 percent is paper or paperboard (cardboard). Think how much longer a landfill could be used if we kept all that paper out of it by recycling.

The average North American uses almost 500 pounds of paper each year, more than people in any other country. In China, for example, people use only about 2 pounds a year. Every scrap is used over and over.

Think about what you throw away each day. Your 1.5 pounds might consist of: a cereal box, 5 sheets of school-work, 3 napkins, a magazine, a newspaper, the box that held your new sneakers, a lunch bag, the packaging from a new toy, and perhaps a candy or gum wrapper.

Probably the only thing that can't be recycled is the packaging from the toy if it is a "bubble" pack. All the other items can be recycled if there are people in the area buying them. Remember that the second arrow in the recycling symbol means that new products are produced from old. Somebody has to find new uses for the fiber in the old paper. But that's not always easy to find.

The magazine, for example, is probably printed on shiny paper with brightly colored photographs. Such paper usually has a clay coating and so can't be recycled with newspaper. However, if you bundle up lots of magazines, you may find a recycler who can take the clay out of the paper.

Some paper you're throwing away may have already been recycled once. Paper napkins are often made from recycled paper. Your school papers may be made of recycled paper. Many states and cities require public institutions to use recycled paper as much as possible.

Look inside a food carton. If it has a gray or tan inner surface, it is made of recycled paper. If it is shiny and white inside, it is made of new wood pulp.

Confusion. Unfortunately, the U.S. federal government has delayed the use of recycled paper through some of its policies. For some years, the U.S. Forest Service has sold timber from national forests at less than it would cost industry to cut it elsewhere. They may have charged only $1 per tree!

This move was meant to encourage the timber industry, but it had bad effects. So many trees were cut down that wildlife habitat was destroyed. And it kept the paper industry relying on virgin (new) fiber instead of on recycled material. That meant that it cost less to use new, freshly cut fiber than to use recycled fiber. Therefore, they haven't built many papermaking plants that use recycled fiber.

Confusion also arises because the word *recycled* does not have a precise meaning. The paper industry has been allowed to say that they were making recycled paper when they included clean paper left over from making rolls of paper. This is industrial waste, called *preconsumer waste*. That paper has never even left the factory!

Earth needs *postconsumer waste* to be used. That's newspapers you read, office paper, and packaging—all of it kept out of the waste stream and recycled.

Making and Remaking Paper

Paper is made from natural fibers, the long, thin strands of cells that make up tree trunks. Originally it was made from cloth rags, but now the fiber usually comes from wood. Some kinds of paper are still made with old textiles—fine stationery has often been made from linen, and your old blue jeans might end up in dollar bills.

In manufacturing paper, water is added to chemically treated wood chips. The resulting *pulp* is beaten until it is broken down into a thick slime and then spread over a screen. The water is then pressed out, leaving a thin sheet of paper as it dries.

It takes 70 percent less energy to make recycled paper than it does to make new paper. A ton of recycled paper uses 7,000 gallons less water, puts 60 pounds less pollution into the air, and produces 3 cubic yards less waste. It also, of course, takes fewer trees—17 fewer trees per ton of paper!

FACT

Paper being recycled is brought to a paper mill in large bales (above). It is then shredded into little pieces (top right) and often mixed with new fiber and water to make a thick paste called pulp (right). The water is removed from the pulp as it feeds through huge rollers that compress and smooth it to make rolls of new paper (below).

Making Your Own Paper

Shred a sheet of newspaper into small pieces. Fill a deep bowl half full of room-temperature water. Mix the paper with the water and let this mixture stand for two hours. In the meantime, locate a smooth, flat piece of clean window screen that will fit into a large, flat pan.

With a hand-operated eggbeater (electric mixers waste energy), break up the fibers. Continue beating until the mixture appears smooth and creamy. Dissolve two tablespoons of cornstarch in half a cup of warm water and stir this solution into your newspaper "soup."

Pour the "soup" into a large, flat pan. Then, slide the window screen into the solution. Pull the screen upward, holding it flat, in order to scoop up a layer of fibers. Hold the screen parallel over the pan until the excess water has dripped out of the pulp. Stir the mixture and dip the screen in it a second or third time, picking up a little more pulp each time. The number of times you dip it will determine the thickness of the paper.

Lay the screen down on a smooth, cloth dish towel. (Don't use paper towels because they cannot be recycled.) Place a sheet of wax paper (not plastic) on top of the screen. Stack several books on top to spread the mixture into a flat, thin sheet. The towel will absorb most of the excess water.

After several minutes, remove the books. Hold the screen flat and carry it outdoors into the sunshine. Find a safe flat place to leave it to dry thoroughly. When it is completely dry, carefully peel your homemade paper off the screen. You can use it to write a letter to a friend.

Papermaking uses a great deal of energy and pollutes a great deal of water. So anything that can save energy and water in papermaking helps the environment. Most paper has been made with some recycled content for many years because it takes less energy to break up the fibers and beat it into the thick slimy material.

Unlike aluminum or glass, paper can be recycled only a few times. It may start as fine office or computer paper. Called "white paper," such high-quality paper is the most valuable for recycling. Then it may become a cheaper grade, perhaps used in a paperback book. Then it may become a box for crackers. And finally, the fiber may be compressed into wallboard and used to build a house. After that, the fiber will never be available for reuse again.

Each time the paper is chopped up for reuse, the long fibers that came from the trees in the first place are broken up more and more, until nothing is left but mush.

Each recycling, however, saves the trees that keep our air clear and cuts down on the chemicals that pollute the huge quantities of water used in papermaking.

"White paper" is high-quality paper, such as the kind used in offices. It is in great demand for recycling.

Paper Cartons. Carton material is called paperboard. The heavy cardboard cartons used for shipping are called corrugated cartons. The middle layer in such cartons is made of rippled—or corrugated—paper that absorbs impact in shipping. Corrugated paper is the easiest paper to recycle and the one that is most often recycled. Grocery stores used to throw shipping cartons out the back door where anyone who was moving could count on finding them. But now most big stores cut up their boxes and sell them to a paperboard recycler. A great deal of American corrugated paperboard is sold to other countries that don't have enough trees.

Two other kinds of paperboard are also made in large quantities. *Bleached* paperboard is used for food containers, especially frozen foods, and *recycled* paperboard is gray or tan inside and used for cereal and cracker boxes.

Newsprint

The United States uses 41 percent of all the special paper called newsprint produced in the world. Newspapers have

It takes 75,000 trees every week to print the Sunday edition of the NEW YORK TIMES.

FACT

During World War II, the Salvation Army helped to collect recyclable material to help the war effort.

The kenaf plant, a relative of cotton, has strong fibers useful in making newsprint that holds ink better, looks brighter, and doesn't turn yellow as quickly as wood-pulp fiber. It may be an answer to saving trees.

long been recycled. Boy Scouts and other organizations have often made extra money and helped the environment by holding "paper drives."

Newspapers use up a lot of trees. You can save a dozen or more full-grown trees every year by recycling your family's newspaper.

Unfortunately, just when more and more people are interested in recycling, the market for recycled newsprint is disappearing—a situation that we hope is temporary.

To help solve the market problem, many states are requiring that newspapers printed within their boundaries include a certain percentage of re-cycled paper. Newsprint has always contained some previously made newsprint, but it was usually the paper left over from manufacturing. The new laws require that newsprint contain recycled newsprint collected from readers, or *postconsumer* newspaper.

Much of the 14 million tons of newsprint

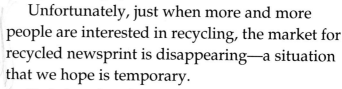

(that's 238 million trees) used in the United States each year comes from Canada. The Canadians don't use anywhere near that amount of newsprint themselves, so the United States will have to ship old newspapers back to Canada for recycling.

One of the major problems with using recycled newspaper (as opposed to waste newsprint that hasn't been printed) is that the ink must be removed. A paper mill that uses recycled paper must have a de-inking process built into it. Several new large paper mills were built in the late 1980s, but only one of them was set up for de-inking paper.

De-inking also causes environmental problems because printing ink has long been a source of toxic heavy metals entering our groundwater. Some newspapers are now using ink made out of soybeans—an organic compound in a water base that can be safely discarded.

Even the passage of twenty years was not enough to make this newspaper decompose in a landfill.

Recycled newsprint also ends up in paperboard, egg cartons, insulation, and even construction paper. And used newspapers are also shredded for use in animal barns instead of straw. It is cheaper and more sterile than hay, and the cows don't seem to mind "because it gives them something to read."

If the increase in recycling continues at its present rate, more than 27 million tons of paper will be recycled in 1992. That's almost half a *billion* trees that won't need to be cut.

Chapter 6

Mines Above Ground

IF WE WANT OUR EARTH TO SURVIVE, we must begin to think of trash as a valuable natural resource and the handling of trash as resource recovery. Day by day, more of the world's people are beginning to accept this viewpoint. In fact, the United States Environmental Protection Agency has set a goal calling for 25 percent of all waste to be recycled by the end of 1992.

To achieve this goal, we must find ways to recycle the trash that comes from people who are unwilling to make the effort to recycle—unfortunately, still far too many people.

In 1990, most places in America are still rescuing just a few items from the trash that end up in the hands of manufacturers who will reuse the materials. Newspapers, as we've seen, must be collected separately or they can't be used. Other recyclables, however, can be separated from each other after they've left home.

Most people are willing to separate recyclables from everything else and put two bags out on the curb. While the nonrecyclable waste is landfilled or incinerated, the other bag of mixed, or commingled, recyclables is taken to *Materials Recovery Facilities,* or MRFs (pronounced "murfs"). Some states refer to them as Intermediate Processing Centers, or IPCs. In these facilities, recyclables are sorted and prepared for shipping to manufacturers.

Entering a Materials Recovery Facility

The trash collection trucks that bring the recyclable mix to the facility back up to an unloading door and dump all the bags or other containers out onto a *tipping floor.*

The bags are broken open by little loading trucks that

gradually push the trash onto a large conveyor belt. Moving from one belt to the next, the trash is gradually spread out so that it is only one item deep. Inspectors along the way look for and remove any items that might harm the machinery, or that might be toxic.

MRF lines that work mostly automatically are called *high tech.* Even high-tech systems, however, have people along the lines to see that everything separates as it should. Systems that use more people to do the labor are called *low tech.* Whichever system is used, the trash is "mined" for all the items that can be recycled.

Steel

Steel is usually the first material to be rescued because it only takes a magnet to remove it from the waste stream. The conveyor belt moves under a large electromagnet. Steel items pop out of the trash and cling to the magnet. The magnet then moves over a bin and releases the items.

Steel , an Old Recyclable. "Salvage for Victory and Be Proud!" said a World War II poster. It meant that people should recycle everything they could to help the war effort. The main item needed was steel—for ships, tanks, and guns.

Americans bought a lot of food in so-called "tin" cans, which are really steel cans with a thin layer of tin to prevent rust and corrosion. After emptying and washing the cans, people would cut out the bottom ends and flatten them. Once a week the cans were taken to a collection point for recycling.

Boys and girls often had special drives to collect scrap metal. Children also earned pennies by collecting steel clothes hangers and returning them to local dry cleaners to be used again. In Europe, almost every big house lost its ornate iron fence and gates, and even its pots and pans, to make weapons of war.

Even after the war was over, steel was still collected because steel furnaces work most efficiently when they have some scrap in them. Scrap dealers continued to collect old cars and appliances.

For 150 years or more, *open-hearth furnaces* used about half scrap metal and about half new molten iron. Scrap iron used in these furnaces brought good prices. But then *basic oxygen furnaces*, which use only about 25 percent scrap,

Old cars provide huge quantities of scrap steel for recycling. Other materials are removed first, then the bodies, engine blocks, and wheels are melted down.

began to be used. The price of scrap went down, and a growing number of old cars were dumped in empty fields around the country.

Fortunately, a new process was started in the 1970s, using an *electric furnace.* This kind of furnace uses intense heat from an electric charge to melt mostly scrap. But today's cars are smaller, and more and more plastic is being used in their bodies, so the price of scrap steel has risen again.

Since World War II, most food cans have just been thrown away. About 5 percent of the waste stream is steel. You can make sure that your cans are reused. Rinse them out, then cut out the closed end of the can. Carefully put both ends back inside the can and crush it flat. Once you have collected many flattened cans, take them to a recycler who handles steel.

FACT

You can run a 60-watt light bulb for over a day on the amount of energy saved by recycling only one pound of steel. In one year in the United States, the recycling of steel saves enough energy to heat and light 18 million homes. Just as important, every ton of recycled steel saves 2,500 pounds of iron ore, 1,000 pounds of coal, and 40 pounds of limestone.

Bimetal Cans. Before aluminum cans became popular for beverages, steel cans were used. Then bimetal cans came on the market. Bimetal cans were made of steel but had an aluminum top for easier opening. They were replaced by the all-aluminum cans. But there is a move to

Heavy equipment and powerful electromagnets are basic needs in a steel recycling center.

bring back the bimetal beverage can, primarily because steel is cheaper than aluminum.

Unfortunately, the new bimetal cans do not have seams like the old ones, so you can't easily tell them from aluminum cans. Soft drinks are often canned locally from syrups shipped by the national company, so the national company may not know whether the local "bottler" uses bimetal cans or not.

An increasing number of recyclers are equipped to handle the separation of steel from aluminum in bimetal cans. But if you have such cans, check with your local recycler before you include them in your collection. You can tell a bimetal can from an aluminum can by placing a small magnet near it. Only steel will be attracted to it.

Huge quantities of aluminum cans are handled at a big Materials Recovery Facility. Aluminum is the most recycled material.

Aluminum

After steel is removed from the commingled trash, the conveyor belt moves over a plate with numerous small holes in it. Small pieces of glass and lead bottle caps fall through the holes and are collected for disposal. The larger items move on. They may go through a curtain made of chain that just brushes the mix. Anything fairly heavy, such as glass, is strong enough to move on through the curtain and drop down into a bin. Lightweight materials, such as plastic bottles and aluminum cans, are brushed onto another belt.

The aluminum and plastic may be separated by sending an electric current through the mass. The aluminum cans take an electric charge so that an electromagnet will pull them off in one direction. The rest of the material is carried on in a different direction. Because this separation process is not always perfect, watchers usually stand ready to pull out items that go in the wrong direction.

Before 1975, most beverages came in glass bottles that were returned to the bottler for sterilizing and refilling. The all-aluminum can was put on the market in 1963 by Reynolds Aluminum, and the first recycling center was started in Los Angeles, California, only five years later. Now, over 80 *billion* aluminum soda and beer cans are made each year. These single-use, one-way containers are an incredible waste of the Earth's resources, unless they are recycled.

At first, people were urged to recycle cans in order to keep them off the roadsides. It was a "nice" thing to do to prevent litter. Now people see that recycling aluminum is vital in protecting the Earth's resources. It takes more oil to make an aluminum can than it does to make almost any other small product. Also, the bauxite ore that yields aluminum is mined mostly from open-pit mines. Such mines damage the ecology of Australia, the Soviet Union, and Guinea, where bauxite is primarily found.

Aluminum manufacturers have come to depend on old cans to make new ones. Almost 60 percent of all cans are now recycled and that number keeps growing as population grows. Aluminum manufacturers have built no new smelting plants (where the alumina from bauxite is separated into aluminum and carbon dioxide, an unwanted by-product that damages the atmosphere), and yet more cans are needed every year. The only way to avoid building new smelters is to keep increasing the number of cans that are recycled.

In Saskatchewan, Canada, which has only recently allowed the sale of aluminum cans, stores must add a 7-cent fee to the purchase of drinks in aluminum cans to cover the cost of recycling. Empty cans are then redeemed for 5 cents at recycling centers, which are often run by disabled people.

It takes 95 percent less energy to make aluminum by recycling it than it does to produce new aluminum from the mineral bauxite. Aluminum beverage cans can be recycled over and over and over again.

Separating aluminum from the rest of the waste simply requires having a separate wastebasket where the empty cans are tossed. In towns that recycle all trash, the cans are bundled up in a bag or box that is picked up separately. Or individuals can sell cans directly to a recycler.

There are about 27 cans to a pound. The highest price ever received (in large railcar bulk) was 76 cents a pound back in 1987. In 1990, an individual walking into a recycler got between 30 and 34 cents a pound.

The price of cans varies with the season—higher in spring when can-makers are preparing for the busy summer cold-drink season, and lowest in the fall. Whatever the season, however, an aluminum can is back on a store shelf only about six weeks after it was sent for recycling.

It is very simple to recycle aluminum cans. They just get chopped into bits and melted to make new sheet aluminum. The ink used to print the cans burns off in the melting process. Some recyclers do the chopping themselves, but they must be careful not to mix in any other metal. A steel can in the melt will damage the equipment.

Any public gathering can benefit from having a can crusher on hand.

Plastics

After an electric current has removed the aluminum from the MRF conveyor belt, plastics of all kinds remain. Operators on the line try to sort the plastic items into the main kinds of plastic so that they can be recycled separately.

Unseparated Plastic. There are more kinds of plastic than there are ways to recognize it, so a lot of plastic is never separated into the different kinds. Instead, scientists are looking for ways to recycle mixed plastic. In Italy, they grind up the commingled plastic and add it to asphalt for road surfaces. As you'll see later, ground-up glass is also used this way, but plastic handles temperature changes even better than glass. The main problem is that there is no way to predict what the mix of plastics will be on any one day, and different mixes have different durability.

The sorting of commingled (mixed) plastics into different types for recycling has to be done by hand.

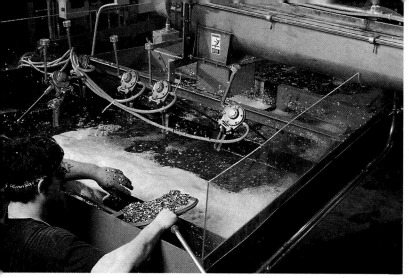

Mixed plastics are shredded and washed (above) *before being melted together and molded into solid objects. Ground-up mixed plastics can be molded into durable and strong outdoor items such as fences* (right).

A great deal of mixed plastic is shipped from the United States to Asia where it is melted and molded into interior parts of toys and other items where the odd colors that might occur do not matter.

Types of Plastic. Plastics are many different kinds of materials made from some of the chemicals in natural gas or crude oil. These basic chemicals are called *polymers*. They consist of many small molecules linked together in gigantic chains. The polymers can be changed into solid form, but they are not easily broken down.

Most plastic (about 87 percent) is of the type called *thermoplastic*. That means that the material becomes soft when it is heated or when pressure is applied, and it hardens when cooled. These plastics are shaped in molds or have gases blown into them to make a product.

The other major type of plastic is called *thermosetting*,

which means that it cannot be softened. Thermosets are used in products that are used over and over, such as dishes or car parts. They can't be melted for use in other products, though they can be shredded. Scientists are trying to break thermosets down into compounds that can be reused.

Of the numerous kinds of plastic used today, only six are commonplace. The plastic container industry has begun to label plastic items to help people separate different kinds of plastic for recycling. The makers put numbers 1 through 7 inside a recycling symbol on the item. You can easily see the symbol on the bottom of a milk bottle or a yogurt container. The number 7 is used for all plastic that does not fit into one of the first six numbers.

Heinz ketchup recently came in a squeeze bottle that made it easier to get the slo-o-o-ow-moving sauce out of the bottle. But the squeeze bottle could not be recycled because it was made out of several layers of different materials—plastics and adhesives—that did different jobs. Heinz has developed a new bottle made of 98.5 percent PET (polyethylene terephthalate). The other tiny percentage consists of a material that keeps oxygen from passing through the plastic, but it has no adhesive and can be recycled as pure PET. (PET is sometimes called PETE because PET is a trade name.)

Styrofoam got a bad reputation when the public first became aware of the damage the chemicals called chlorofluorocarbons (CFCs) were causing to the Earth's ozone layer. The chlorine in CFCs was released into the upper atmosphere where it reacted with ozone, making the Earth's ozone layer thinner. Without the ozone layer, too much ultraviolet light from the sun would strike Earth, causing severe sunburn and skin cancer.

RECYCLING YOUR PLASTICS

1
PETE

3
PVC

2
HDPE

5
PP

6
PS

7
OTHER

NAME	USED FOR	RECYCLING PROCESS
♳ 1 Polyethylene Terephthalate (PET, often called "PETE")	Clear tops of 2-liter plastic soda bottles, food product bottles, disposable glasses	Cleaned and processed into flakes. Made into soda bottles, other types of bottles, carpeting, and paint brushes. Shredded into fiber, and used as the fluff in fiber-filled coats and sleeping bags
♴ 2 High Density Polyethylene (HDPE)	Dark-colored bottoms of soda bottles, milk and water jugs, shampoo and detergent bottles, reusable drinking cups	Cleaned and processed into flakes. Made into milk and water jugs, trash cans, drainage pipes, and containers used to sort recyclables. Also turned into long, strong fibers used in bullet-proof vests
♵ 3 Vinyl/Polyvinyl Chloride (PVC)	Film for wrapping meat; bottles for edible oils, water and liquor; plumbing pipes; molded plastic furniture	All other recyclables are usually mixed together and ground up. The plastic bits are cleaned, heated, poured into large molds, and cooled. This mix is made into such items as plastic lumber, picnic tables, sand boxes, stadium seats, fencing, pallets, storage bins, park benches, car barriers, farm pens for poultry and pigs, seawalls, lobster traps, compost enclosures, golf course walkways, and playground equipment
♶ 4 Low Density Polypropylene (LDPE)	Coffee-can lids, 6-pack rings	
♷ 5 Polypropylene (PP)	Yogurt containers, screw tops, snap-on lids	
♸ 6 Polystyrene (PS)	Foam packaging for sandwiches, meat trays, disposable hot-drink cups, packing peanuts, egg cartons, insulation	
♹ 7 All Other Resins and Layered Materials (OTHER)	Squeeze bottles for some ketchups, sauces, syrups and jellies; molded office supplies; small food tubs	

CFCs are used to make liquid polystyrene expand into foam. However, they are being replaced by safer chemicals that don't react with ozone so quickly.

One of the best-known users of polystyrene foam has been McDonald's restaurant chain. In 1987, McDonald's stopped buying Styrofoam packaging made with CFCs and switched to a safer chemical called HCFC. But they continued using polystyrene boxes. In 1990 the company began recycling polystyrene, but by the end of the year they had decided to stop using plastic packaging.

The Problem with Plastics. Many people think that plastic is one of the biggest dangers to our environment because it lasts so long and its useful life is very short. A "clamshell" container at a fast-food restaurant, for example, may hold a hamburger for the few minutes it takes a customer to walk to a seat and eat his meal. Then the container is thrown away. A plastic milk bottle might stay at a grocery store for three days before the milk is bought and consumed, and the plastic bottle is discarded. A plastic toy might be used for a year before it breaks. On the other hand, plastic siding might keep a house carefree, protected, and looking nice for twenty years.

Whatever the item's useful life, however, the plastic may last hundreds of years in a landfill. Plastic molecules are not like the ones made by nature, and they are not broken down by bacteria as natural materials are. In addition, plastic takes up considerable room in a landfill. Of the trash we throw away, only 7 percent by weight is plastic, mainly packaging of various kinds. However, that 7 percent takes up 20 percent of the room in our solid-waste stream.

Some plastics are a danger to animal life in lakes and oceans. The rings that hold six-pack cans together can strangle an animal. Other animals accidentally eat plastic bags, which can stop up their digestive systems.

Making Plastics Decompose. Some states have tried to pass laws prohibiting the use of plastic, but that is no real solution either. The results would not necessarily be helpful to people. Medical supplies, for example, would cost much more than they do if they had to be collected, washed, and sterilized for reuse, as they used to be. Plastic disposables are safer and cheaper. Our food supplies last longer, with less waste, than they would without plastic.

The solution is to make plastics that behave like materials that break down.

Nature decomposes only those molecules that it makes—and it doesn't make plastic molecules. Thus plastics don't disintegrate easily. Scientists are working on ways to make plastic decompose, or degrade—or at least to be less resistant to biological decomposition.

Some manufacturers have added cornstarch to the plastic used in plastic bags to make them *biodegradable*. Cornstarch is a natural polymer that mixes with the plastic. But once the 8 to 10 percent of the bag material that is cornstarch has degraded, the remainder of the plastic item still exists on the ground or in a landfill.

Some plastics have been developed that are *photodegradable*—they break down in the presence of sunlight. This kind of plastic would not degrade at all in a dark landfill. However, it could be chopped up and spread on farm fields as mulch, where it would decompose in the light and become part of the soil. It would not harm plants or animals.

Some European manufacturers are working on plastics that will decompose when another chemical is added to them. The plastic materials could be collected by normal recycling methods. Then when the chemical is added, they break down into the original polymers.

Several polymers made in nature, called *biopolymers*, have been discovered. Cornstarch is one. A manufacturer of over-the-counter drug products has developed a plastic made of a starch base instead of a petroleum base. Scientists hope to be able to use this plastic in products that are apt to end up in places where they endanger wildlife. If such products degrade fairly quickly after use (but not before they are bought), they will be less dangerous to animals.

Lexan is a recyclable polycarbonate plastic from General Electric Company that can be made into milk bottles (below). The bottles can be washed and refilled up to 100 times before the plastic is recycled into lightweight, inexpensive auto parts (right). Even those can be reclaimed and turned into wall panels that will be in place for many years.

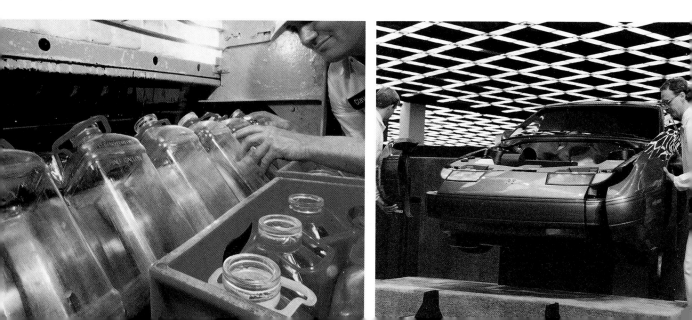

Glass should be separated into the three colors of green, brown, and clear for recycling. Broken or mixed glass can be crushed for use in asphalt road surfaces.

Glass

Glass that remains on the conveyor belt after the lighter materials are removed is carried on to a glass-separating section. If the glass is just to be crushed into tiny bits called *cullet*, the colors of glass are not separated. However, if the glass is being sold for melting down, the three main colors of glass—clear (which is called *flint* glass), amber (also called brown), and green—must be separated.

In most MRFs, an inspector wearing gloves separates the three colors. However, in newer facilities a special optical machine inspects each bottle, reads the color, and sends a signal to a set of tongs. The tongs pick up the bottle and deposit it in a bin with others of the same color.

Some types of glass should not be mixed with the bottles we send for recycling. Pyrex, the glass used for baking, for example, has been treated so that it will not melt. Glass used in windows is made from a different formula than container glass. Light bulbs have metal parts that could mess up the recycling machinery. And ceramics, such as china dishes or statues, are not glass and therefore should not be included.

When preseparating glass at home, you don't need to remove paper labels. They burn off when the glass is melted. But plastic neck rings or metal caps should all be removed

The glass recycling symbol

The ingredients in recycled glass (right)— *sand, ash, limestone, and cullet—are melted together and blown into new bottles* (above).

before you put bottles out with the other trash for recycling.

Most glass manufacturers use about 25 percent cullet (small crushed pieces) mixed with melted sand, soda ash, and limestone when making new glass containers. A growing number, however, are beginning to use as much as 80 percent cullet or even more.

In 1972, Oregon became the first state to have a "bottle bill"—a law requiring that all glass, aluminum, and plastic drink bottles be returned for recycling. Buyers of soft drinks, for example, are required to pay a few cents deposit for each bottle. When they return the empty containers to the store, they get their deposit back.

While 90 percent of all glass containers sent for recycling end up as new containers, some glass is used instead of pebbles to provide the hard content of asphalt road surfaces. Cities, where lots of glass is available and lots of roads need regular resurfacing, are using a lot of *glasphalt,* as the material is called.

Baltimore, Maryland, has used glasphalt for twenty years on roads in downtown areas where traffic does not move fast. They also use it in parking lots. It is rarely used on residential streets because pieces of glass often separate out.

The main advantage of glasphalt, besides using up waste glass, is that it dries faster than regular asphalt. It also retains heat longer, so that the surface does not ice up as quickly in winter.

Reaching the End of the MRF

In most Materials Recovery Facilities, we've now reached the end of the conveyor belt line. All of the recyclables have been collected into separate bins. Now they may be handled again in some way—for example, the glass may be crushed or the aluminum shredded. They are then baled up for shipment to the appropriate manufacturers, where the materials begin a new life.

At the end of the Materials Recovery Facility, the different materials have been collected and baled for shipment. These crushed and baled aluminum cans will be delivered to a beverage-can maker who will make the metal into more cans.

Chapter 7

Oil, Tires,
Odds and Ends

THERE ARE, OF COURSE, SOME ITEMS that can be recycled that do not fit into the usual municipal waste. If they are found in the trash at a Materials Recovery Center, they will usually be tossed aside to be dealt with separately. Some of the items are among the biggest that people throw away.

Appliances

Major household appliances, which are called *white goods* by the recycling industry, are very useful for their steel, and they are often recycled. However, there are problems with recycling old refrigerators and air conditioners.

The first problem is that the Freon gas used in refrigeration units contains chlorofluorocarbons—chemicals that are damaging Earth's atmosphere. In the past, the cooling tubes of a discarded refrigerator were just opened up and the gas was allowed to escape into the air.

Appliances of the future will have a different, safer gas in the cooling tubes, but old appliances will still be around and will still need to be repaired or disposed of. The Freon gas now must be collected from old appliances and cleaned and filtered for reuse.

A second problem exists with older appliances—stoves, refrigerators, air conditioners, dishwashers, dryers, washers, and trash compactors. These items were made with motor parts that contain polychlorinated biphenyls (PCBs). These chemicals are fluids that prevent electrical overloading in the equipment, so that it doesn't catch on fire.

In the 1970s, PCBs were shown to cause cancer in the people who worked with them. In the 1980s these chemicals were no longer used in appliances. However, firms that

Old appliances are torn apart and their insulation removed before the steel is shredded for use in new steel (above). Tires are also shredded (right) for a variety of uses, including road or playground surfaces and incineration.

recycled older appliances were found to have a high incidence of cancer among their employees. Now there are companies that remove the dangerous capacitors, along with electric switches that contain mercury, and other items that the metal scrap dealers cannot handle. The firms that remove these items handle them as hazardous waste before selling the steel to a metal recycler.

Tires

There are millions upon millions of cars and trucks on the roads of the world, and all of them have at least four tires. Each vehicle has its tires changed two or three times during its useful life. Something has to be done with those billions of old tires. There are far too many to use them all as swings, boat bumpers, or sand piles.

In the past, many auto tires were sent to have a new tread—the molded outside layer—put on them. But that number has dropped to fewer than 10 percent of all passenger-car tires being retreaded. Many more truck, bus, and airplane tires are retreaded because they are so expensive.

Many tires end up in city dumps or in landfills. But

there's something about rubber tires—they don't want to stay put. Because the rubber can't be compressed and because there is usually air caught inside the rubber cylinder, tires tend to rise up out of trash heaps and "float" to the surface.

Some tires end up in special tire dumps, where people pay to leave their old tires. These mountains of rubber are getting bigger and bigger. There are probably two billion tires stockpiled around the United States, with another billion in Canada. They attract rodents and insects.

Frequently the mountains of discarded tires are set on fire, either accidentally or on purpose. In February 1989, near Toronto, Canada, a dump containing at least fourteen million tires caught on fire. It took seventeen days for the firemen to extinguish the blaze. In the meantime, the burning rubber gave off horrible, oily, toxic, black smoke that filled the air for hundreds of miles.

In Virginia in 1984, a smaller dump burned for nine months before the fire was put out. The air was affected in four states, and the groundwater beneath Virginia is still contaminated. The ground is contaminated with zinc, an ingredient in tire rubber.

Tires are made of synthetic rubber rather than the natural rubber that is the product of the South American plant called *Hevea brasiliensis*, or the rubber tree. Like plastic, synthetic rubber is a petroleum-based polymer. About five gallons of oil are used in making the rubber for one tire. This rubber is used to coat various other materials, such as steel reinforcing, nylon cords, and fiberglass belts. These variations—plus the fact that tires are made to be long-lasting—make recycling them very difficult.

At least 250 million tires—one for every American—are discarded in the United States each year. Currently, not more than 5 percent of old tires are recycled.

Sometimes the outer rubber cap of an old tire is removed and flattened to make flat rubber items such as doormats, shoe soles, and gaskets. In poorer countries of the world, such rubber is cut into sections and used as sandals. A diligent sandal maker can get three pairs of shoes from one tire.

Tires are also being used in piles under soil to create berms—the ridges of land placed between housing developments and major highways to cut noise. Tires can also be spread over the ground to prevent soil erosion or the washing out of river embankments. They can be anchored in rivers and lakes to attract fish.

Some companies are putting old tires through a process called pyrolysis in which the tires are heated without oxygen—and without burning—until the rubber breaks down into its chemical components. Pyrolysis captures oil, natural

gas, carbon black, steel, and fabric for reuse in other products.

Even more tires are being incinerated, or burned with oxygen, as fuel. The energy value of tires is at least 50 percent higher than that of coal. Shredded tires burn very hot, making other fuel used with them burn better than it otherwise would.

Old tires can be finely chopped and mixed with other materials to make a safe, comfortable playing surface for children.

Perhaps the biggest tire dump in the world—at least 35 million tires—is located near Modesto, California. A New York company called Oxford Energy has built an energy production plant (shown on page 94) near the dump that uses chopped-up tires (called TDF, for *tire-derived fuel*) as its fuel. The plant generates enough electricity to power 14,000 nearby homes and uses up 5 million tires a year. The fire burns at such a high temperature—2300° F.—that no dirty smoke is given off to pollute the air.

Some people think that tires should be landfilled after all. Someday, when petroleum prices are even higher than they are now, the tires will still be there in reserve. Then people might be more willing to have them incinerated for energy.

Driving to Save Tires

Keep the correct air pressure in your tires.
Drive smoothly, avoiding sudden stops, quick starts, or abrupt turns.
Be sure all the wheels are kept aligned and balanced.
Avoid rough roads, and keep an eye out for potholes.
When there's 1/16 inch of tread left (or the tread reaches the "wear bar" marked on the tire) send it for retreading.

Motor Oil

Every car must have its oil changed regularly so that the engine will run smoothly and use less gas. In the United States, more than 700 million gallons of motor oil are used each year. But what do we do with the old oil?

For almost a hundred years, people who changed their own oil just dumped the old oil in some convenient spot—a stream, along the roadside, into an unused spot in the garden, into a storm drain on the street, or into lots of newspaper and rags and then into the trash. Or sometimes they poured the dirty, sludgy substance into a bottle and threw the bottle into the trash.

Motor oil as it comes for recycling is thick and black. After being strained and purified, it is ready for reuse.

None of those methods was any good. The oil always ended up polluting water. Only one part oil in one million parts of water (a unit called 1 part per million, or 1 ppm) can make water taste and smell peculiar. Only 35 ppm actually shows up as an oil slick on the water that can harm living things.

FACT

The dirty oil from only one oil change for one car if dumped in a pond or allowed into groundwater can ruin a million gallons of water—a year's supply for fifty people!

Used oil contains elements that can cause cancer if people regularly drink water containing them. They can kill fish. They can destroy life in a patch of ground. And, of course, old oil must be replaced by new oil.

Fortunately, motor oil can be recycled. Major service stations have been doing it for years. But many car drivers change the oil in their cars themselves, instead of having it done in a service station. A person changing his or her own oil must use a little more effort to finish the task by recycling the oil. Many service stations will recycle oil from individual car owners.

Textiles

When you throw away a torn shirt or blouse, you don't think about the fact that you're actually discarding textiles, many of which could be used again.

In the old days of not so long ago, worn-out clothing was recycled into usable products by skillful mothers and grandmothers. The family slept under homemade quilts. The floor was covered with rugs made from thin strips of worn-out clothing braided together and sewn into big circles.

Such crafts have become important again in recent years, though now they are done more as a relaxing hobby than a necessity. However, if no one in your family is involved in such hobbies, perhaps you can find someone who is. Give that person your old clothing to use.

These Canadian women show that quilt-making is a social occasion as well as a good way to reuse textiles.

Take a good look at any clothes your family might be considering throwing away. Perhaps a worn collar can be turned around to look new. Collar turning used to be a regular business in big cities. Is the pocket of your pants worn through on the inside? You can buy replacement pockets and make the pants like new again. If the top of a dress is worn through, could you make a skirt from it?

These are all sewing tasks that perhaps you—whether you're a boy or a girl—can learn to do in a sewing class or a Scout group.

If you can't sell your unwanted clothing at a garage sale, give it to an organization that makes a business of recycling clothing and household items for the needy.

Batteries

Almost 3 billion pounds of batteries are thrown away by Americans each year. They might be the big black liquid-filled (lead-acid) car batteries or the small dry-cell batteries used in radios and flashlights. Whichever they are, they should not be just thrown into the trash because they contain materials that are both valuable and dangerous. Household batteries may contain zinc, silver, mercury, cadmium, lead, lithium, manganese, and nickel. All of these minerals must be taken from the Earth, and many of them are toxic if they get into our water supplies.

One battery maker described batteries as "little packages of chemicals." Several of the chemicals are carcinogenic, or cancer-causing. Mercury, one of the main carcinogens, is added to batteries to make the other chemicals stable—not apt to explode. In recent years, the amount of mercury used for this purpose has been lessened considerably. Some batteries are made with no mercury.

Many environmentalists believe that batteries placed in a landfill will eventually break up and release their toxic contents into the soil and water. However, these days they are likely to be sent to an incinerator. When burned, they may release these elements into the air. The ash, which is also heavy in these dangerous metals, must still be put into a landfill.

Several countries and some states require that all batteries be recycled by the manufacturers, who extract the metals and reuse them in new batteries. The lead, the plastic knobs, and the acid of lead-acid batteries can all be recycled. In the United States, Washington State requires a customer buying a lead-acid car battery to pay a $5 recycling fee unless he brings in an old battery to be recycled. The state of Maine charges a $10 deposit.

Many of the items in our society these days use dry-cell batteries. Before you buy such a toy or appliance or radio, you might seriously consider whether you want to add to the battery-using devices in your life. If you do, buy rechargeable nickel-cadmium batteries. Yes, you have to buy the recharger, too, but you'll save money in the long run. You can recharge these batteries up to one hundred times instead of replacing them every few weeks.

As you replace older batteries with newer rechargeable ones, store the old ones until your town has a collection day for hazardous or toxic household waste.

The catalytic converter serves to prevent some pollutants in automobile exhaust from being put into the air. The converter can be removed from an old car in order to recycle the precious metals used in it.

Chapter 8

Recycling in Your Community

EVERY TOWN, VILLAGE, OR CITY is different. Each has its own atmosphere. That's why people choose a particular area to live in. But they all have at least one thing in common—the government must provide for the pickup and disposal of trash. If they didn't, people would not want to live there.

Trash-collection trucks go through different areas of town on different days, so that everybody's trash is collected at least once a week. Perhaps you've had to help take the week's accumulation of trash out to the curb for pickup. After collecting the trash, the trucks usually take it to a dump or landfill where the trash is tipped in.

If you live in an apartment, you've probably had to take trash to a central collection room. Perhaps your apartment building has an "incinerator room" on each floor, where trash is dumped down a chute right into a furnace for heating the building.

All over North America—in fact, all over the world—our ways of getting rid of trash are beginning to change. What is happening in your community?

Milwaukee, Wisconsin, provides three different bins, often called igloos, for collecting three different colors of glass for recycling.

An Earth Experience

Finding Out about Your Community

Your concern for the environment starts in your own home and in your own community. If you don't already know how trash is handled in your town or city, you can easily find out.

First, think about what you already know. Have you seen garbage trucks rumbling through the streets? What day is your trash put out on the curb? Have you ever helped take an old couch or some other large piece of furniture to a dump? Did you have to pay to dump it?

Is there a big building in your town with smokestacks that seem to soar into the air? Perhaps it's an incinerator. Is the incinerator a waste-to-energy *type, being used to produce heat for making electricity, or is it a* mass-burn *incinerator that burns all solid waste? See what you can find out about it.*

Now it's time to get answers to things you don't know. You might start by calling the municipal government offices, usually the city hall or town hall. Ask if your community does any recycling, or if there are any plans for it. Even if the municipality itself does not yet organize recycling, the town officials probably would know if some volunteer organization in town collects for recycling. Frequently, there will be just aluminum, or just newspaper, or just plastic bottles being collected. Many towns now also collect white paper.

If you can get into a really good conversation with the official on the phone, you might try to find out how much the town pays to have garbage collected (of course, the homeowners actually pay the taxes or fees). If the town recycles, what is the officials' attitude toward paying to have recyclables kept out of the waste stream? Does the town expect to earn money through recycling or will it pay to eliminate certain items from the landfill it uses?

Look in the Yellow Pages *under "Garbage Disposal" or "Rubbish Removal." Call the numbers you see listed there. Tell the person who answers what you are trying to learn and ask if he or she can answer some questions for you. You might try to find out:*

How much trash is collected each week?

Is any of it separated for recycling?

How is it separated?

Who buys the recyclables?

What industries in town create a lot of waste?

What kind of waste is it and where is it taken?

Is any of the industrial waste recycled?

Where is the trash from your town taken?

If the town recycles, what happens to the remaining material that can't easily be separated?

How much longer do they think the local landfill will be usable?

Is there room to build another one if the current landfill reaches capacity?

Is trash from any other area brought into the landfill closest to you?

If there is a Materials Recovery Facility anywhere near you, perhaps you could visit it and see it in action. Is it anything like the one described in Chapter 7? It will probably use more people and fewer machines to do the work of separation. Or it might be even more high tech.

The questions that you ask just go on and on, because trash plays such an important role in the way we live today . . . and the way we live creates so much trash.

Laws about Recycling

The collection of waste for recycling decreased after World War II. Most people forgot about it except on those annual occasions when the local Boy Scouts or another group had a newspaper drive.

Recycling itself, however, never stopped. Almost every community still had its "scrap dealer" who collected old appliances, automobiles, and other metals for reselling to steel and aluminum manufacturers. They were the ones who bought and resold the mountains of newsprint that the Boy Scouts collected. But few people were aware that such dealers existed.

In the late 1960s, some people began to be aware that the environment was getting into trouble. Activists started recycling on a small scale. They found the scrap buyers and set up collection points for the few people who cared. And they tried to convince other people to join them in recycling.

The city of Madison, Wisconsin, started a program of newspaper collection in 1968. This effort gave the city some extra money that helped pay for their garbage collection, and it kept newspapers out of the landfills.

When the first Earth Day was held in 1970, more people became aware that waste was a major problem. Hundreds, even thousands, of recycling centers were set up—at least for a little while. Many volunteers lost interest, however, when it became difficult to get the material collected, or if they lost their storage space, or shipping cost too much.

Enough people continued to care, however, for lawmakers to begin to feel the pressure. In 1972 the state of Vermont just barely passed a "bottle bill" requiring a deposit on all beer and soda bottles. It did pass, though, and it passed by

On Earth Day 1990, children in Richmond, Virginia, became "garbologists" by separating 1/3 ton of waste into items that can be recycled and those that cannot.

an even larger margin the following year when some citizens who didn't like the extra "work" of returning bottles tried to get the law repealed.

One thing became clear as the years went on: mandatory recycling—that is, recycling required by law—was a lot more effective than voluntary recycling. So people began to put more effort into getting the laws changed in their communities and states.

In California, laws were passed that required towns without a recycling program to pay more for dumping their trash in landfills than recycling towns had to pay.

As part of the Richmond project, students created a display on the time it takes various materials to decompose.

Jersey City, New Jersey, became the largest city with mandatory recycling and "police" to back up the law. Garbage at the curb is regularly inspected on a random basis by the "garbage police." Citizens who fail to put recyclable material out for separate collection can be fined.

Cities, however, can do only so much. Gradually, more and more state governments have become involved in recycling. By 1990, at least 37 states had passed recycling laws, and most others were considering them.

The United States Environmental Protection Agency made rules that the states must follow by changing their own laws. One of these outlawed the use of the old-fashioned rural town dump by June 1990. Many towns with dumps that polluted their groundwater had to build sanitary landfills or take their garbage to another community's landfill. A landfill that meets EPA requirements is estimated to cost about $50 million to build.

Another EPA regulation set a goal requiring all communities in the United States to separate 25 percent of their trash into recyclables by the end of 1992.

Passing Laws Is Not Enough

It's all very well for a community to collect recyclables, but what good does it do if there is nowhere to sell them? One big city in Minnesota set up a legally required newspaper recycling program and then ended up dumping the newspaper collected into landfills anyway, because no one was buying newsprint at that particular time. Many citizens, angry that their efforts had been worthless, didn't recycle again for a long time.

States must make sure that there are buyers for the material collected. That can happen only if laws are passed requiring the use of recycled material. For example, Connecticut has passed a law requiring any newspaper sold within its borders to be printed on newsprint containing a certain percentage of old newspapers. Many states require government offices to use recycled paper.

RecycleSaurous™ *is a character created by Creative Printing and Publishing to encourage people to recycle.*

If every state required the use of recycled papers or other materials, there would be competition among the buyers of recyclables and prices would increase. Individuals may not make money directly from recycling, but they will probably pay less tax for trash collection in their municipalities. Some states are making low-interest loans available to companies that buy recycled materials.

Also, states must cooperate with each other. For example, in New England, the states are working together to acquire a de-inking mill for the region.

Another state regulation that will have an effect on all of us is a ban on yard waste in landfills. Many people think that the solution is to return to burning leaf piles in our own yards, but the burning of organic matter puts carbon dioxide into the atmosphere. Carbon dioxide is contributing to the

"Recycling Pete" (above) is a dancing 2-liter bottle that urges consumers to recycle. PETE is an alternative name for PET, or polyethylene terephthalate. PET bottles are flaked and then puffed into fiberfill (right), which can be used to stuff pillows and warm vests.

global warming problem. The only real answer is composting, both on a private basis in your own yard and on a municipal basis.

"Environmentally Friendly" Buying

In the United States, Canada, and many European countries, there is lots of interest in "green consumerism"—the name given to buying goods based on what is best for the environment. The more people demand environmentally friendly products, the more such products there will be on the market.

Very soon the United States will have a nationally recognized program of labeling goods as to their recyclability or the fact that they are made out of recycled materials. Right now, many firms are putting the recycling symbol on their packages, but there are no requirements that force companies to meet certain standards of recyclability or the use of recycled materials before they can use the symbol. Consumers become confused about all the differing claims that companies make in their advertising.

Some other countries have developed strict symbol programs. In Germany, for example, the "Blue Angel" program has been in effect since 1978. It is a government-run program in which products earn the right to carry a label indicating that the product is environmentally friendly (or at least helps reduce waste, because nothing is truly environmentally friendly). Mercury-free batteries are an example of a product that carries the German symbol, which is an adaptation of the United Nations symbol.

One of the bases for being awarded the label by a special commission is that products contain recycled materials. Because most paper contains some recycled paper and always has, a paper product in Germany receives the Blue Angel label only if it contains 100-percent recycled, post-consumer paper.

Japan has a similar program with a symbol that shows stylized arms holding the Earth. Its meaning is "Let's save the Earth with our own hands."

Canada's program is a joint effort among the government, industry, and consumers. Like the United States' recycling symbol, it has three parts, but instead of arrows, the parts are doves, making the symbol look very like Canada's maple leaf symbol.

In coming years, many more countries will probably develop similar programs to indicate the environmental friendliness of products. Also, because we are one world and what one country does affects other countries, it is probable that eventually an international agreement of some sort will be reached. Then we will truly be saving the Earth.

Chapter 9
"Yes, But . . ."

MANY PEOPLE WHO CARE about the environment have become involved in recycling because it is something that each one of us can do to help the Earth here and now. That's important, but unfortunately, it's not the whole picture.

Just as everything in nature is a matter of balance, everything to do with recycling and environmental concerns is also a matter of balance, and of making choices. And when someone makes a choice, there's always someone else who would have made a different choice . . . and have good reasons for doing so. For example:

We need to collect and recycle as much paper as we can, and all of us should be buying recycled paper.

Yes, but if we do that, thousands of lumbermen could lose their jobs.

We could answer:*Yes, but* if they lose their jobs in lumbering, they could be retrained to work in the growing recycling industries.

The Diaper Issue

An environment-related choice that millions of mothers and fathers have to make is whether or not to use disposable diapers on their babies. When disposable diapers first came on the market, parents breathed a sigh of relief that they no longer had to collect dirty cloth diapers and wash them themselves or collect them to be washed by others.

Disposable diapers are wonderfully easy to use: take off the dirty one, throw it away, wash the baby's bottom, and put on a clean diaper.

But before a baby gets into underpants, he or she will use up perhaps 10,000 diapers. Making these diapers uses many

A baby wearing cloth diapers would use only a few dozen during infancy, but one who wears disposable diapers would send thousands of them to landfills during the same period.

barrels of oil for the plastic outer coating and the gel of acrylic crystals that absorbs liquid. In addition, many millions of trees are cut down for the absorbent wood-pulp fluff that is still used in many diapers. And, of course, when they're thrown away, they do not just disappear. They lie there in landfills and create more leachate and methane gas.

It seems easy to say, "Well, just go back to using cloth diapers." Many parents are willing to do that, especially when they see how much cheaper it is. One researcher has shown that a cloth diaper washed at home costs 3 cents per use. A cloth diaper washed by a diaper service costs 13 cents per use. And a disposable diaper costs about 22 cents per use. Cloth diapers have the advantage that the waste that collects in them is disposed of in the toilet, washing machine, and sewage treatment plant instead of in landfills.

Yes, but cloth diapers create their own problems. The sewage treatment loads are heavier. The water used for washing is greater. The energy used by services to sterilize the diapers and to pick up and deliver them has to be counted in.

Yes, but the energy costs of transporting the diapers as garbage and the fact that they can't be recycled outweighs those considerations.

What choice would you make if you were a parent?

Making Business Choices

A solid-waste-management professional has said: "Industry in North America is permitted to develop any product it chooses, package it any way it wishes, and never have to take any responsibility for how that product impacts either on the amount of solid waste generated or on the availability of natural resources."

In the past, few people wanted to see business conducted differently. But now our planet is hurting. Now, if enough people—you included—want to see business conducted differently, we have to let the people who make business decisions know that we want to see limits placed on what they can do—limits that would protect our environment.

For example, every time a new shampoo, lotion, or other liquid product comes on the market, the designers of the packaging want to be sure that it will catch your attention in the store. They might give the bottle a special color, they might give it an unusual shape—anything to catch your eye and make you pick it up.

Some countries, however, have decreed that all bottles must be made in a few standardized shapes and sizes. Then, instead of having to use resources to sort the glass, break it, melt it, and remold it into new shapes, the bottles are simply washed and reused. The most energy-efficient and resource-saving containers are refillable glass bottles. But do we have the right to take away freedom of choice from individuals?

It's important that each of us no longer view the cost of a product as just the "$5.95" shown on the price tag of, for example, a plastic toy car. As part of the cost we must include the oil used in making the plastic that is gone forever, as well as the cost of disposing of the packaging and the cost to the environment if the final, broken car has to be landfilled. We can't yet put a number on those costs, but they are just as real as the one on the price tag.

Each of us has to balance out those costs for ourselves and make our own decisions.

Looking at the "Pros" and "Cons." Early in 1990, two big American companies made decisions that affect some foods we eat. More particularly, they made decisions about the packages they come in—the aseptic box, or drink box, used by the Coca-Cola Company for single servings of Minute Maid juices, and the polystyrene foam "clamshell" box used by some fast-food restaurants to hold their hamburgers and other sandwiches. Public protest against the foam boxes mounted after people found out about the danger of CFCs. McDonald's, for example, had the manufacturers of their boxes change the chemical they used. They continued to use foam boxes until 1991.

On the following two pages, we present the "Pros" (facts in favor) and "Cons" (facts against) on these two issues as they affect the environment. Read both sides of the argument carefully.

If you were the corporate executive having to make the decision, how would you decide on these two issues?

You are a consumer. What will you decide about buying these products?

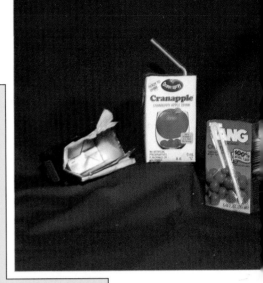

The Aseptic Juice Box

Pros

- It is lightweight, unbreakable, and safe.
- It is fun to drink from.
- Because it is rectangular, it packs tightly and compactly for both shipping (thus reducing transportation fuel usage and pollution) and storing.
- The contents do not have to be heated when packed, thus preserving flavor and saving energy.
- It does not require refrigeration, thus saving energy.
- The energy required to make it is about half that needed to make a 10-ounce glass bottle.
- When incinerated, 70 percent of the energy required to make the package is recovered.
- It requires the least packaging in proportion to weight of contents of any package.
- The package is inert in a landfill and so does not produce polluting leachate.

Cons

- The combination of materials used in making it prevents it from being recycled except in a shredded mixture.
- The containers it replaces (steel and aluminum) can be recycled.
- The plastic and aluminum layers it contains are made from nonrenewable resources.
- The package will not decompose in a landfill for many decades.

The Styrofoam Box

Pros

• It keeps food moister and hotter than a paper box.

• It is technically possible to recycle it, and for a while in 1990 McDonald's collected the boxes in some stores for recycling.

• It is a single material, whereas the probable substitute—plastic-coated paper— is not recyclable.

• It is more sanitary than washable, reusable plates.

• It saves trees.

• It requires less energy than paper to make.

• It compresses in a landfill, thus taking up less room.

• When incinerated, it burns at a high temperature, thus burning all trash around it hotter and cleaner.

Cons

• Food eaten at the restaurants does not need to be kept hot and moist; valuable resources are being wasted for a minute or so of use.

• Only a few places are recycling polystyrene foam; in most places the box ends up in a landfill.

• When the box is discarded away from the restaurant, there is little likelihood that it will be recycled.

• When thrown away outdoors, it does not decompose.

• Polystyrene uses up nonrenewable resources.

• The gases used in making polystyrene can be dangerous to the atmosphere.

Most companies do not give us as much information about the decisions that went into their products as Coca-Cola and McDonald's have. But you still have to try to figure out all the "yes, buts" for any product in order to make good, environmentally sound decisions when you shop. Ask yourself:

Does the manufacturing of the product hurt the environment or the people who work at the factory?

Is it packaged in such a way that I have to get rid of more waste than the product is worth to me?

If I use the product, will I be harming the air, the water, the land, or the people around me?

When I'm through with the product, can it be used further by other people?

When everyone is through with it, can the materials be recycled?

In the future, packaging will need to be designed to take into consideration the effects on the environment of its manufacture, transportation, and disposal.

Chapter 10
Taking Action

IN ORDER FOR OUR PLANET TO RETURN to being a safe, productive, beautiful, and varied home for us all, we must all do what we can to help rescue it. The time is past when we can say, "Well, someday someone will figure out what to do about the problems." The environmentalists have told us what needs doing, and it needs doing now.

Whatever age you are, you can start taking action to help the Earth. You learned many ways to do that while reading the pages of this book. Maybe you think that there's not much point in trying unless your family and friends try, too—and they don't seem very concerned. But all you can do is change the way *you* take care of your little corner of the planet by cleaning up the waste around you, and making sure that it gets recycled. Just keep hoping that others, seeing you take action, will do so, too.

The following lists suggest ways you can take action to protect our natural resources and clean up our waste—reduce, reuse, recycle, and compost, or 3RC. Some of the suggestions are reminders of things you read in this book, some are general suggestions for ways to live your life with concern for the environment, and others are guidelines for expressing your opinion to people who make environmental policy.

Taking Personal Action

The most important thing any one of us can do is make sure that our own home is environmentally friendly, that our waste does not contribute to Earth's problems. Help everyone you know to become a shopper who is always conscious of the environment.

One example of a convenient recycling arrangement in the cabinets below your kitchen counter or sink.

1. Keep 3RC in mind at all times—

REDUCE, REUSE, RECYCLE, COMPOST!

2. Set up your home for easy recycling. Put separate containers for recyclables in easy reach. Use washable, plastic wastebaskets that you can put trash in directly instead of having to line them with plastic or paper, unless you are filling plastic bags with plastic and paper bags with newspapers.

3. Establish a compost pile in your backyard. Carry fresh garbage to it every day (but keep the meat and oils out of it), turning the new material inside the old. Use the resulting humus instead of chemical fertilizer to fertilize your garden.

4. Pack environmental lunches for yourself. Put sandwiches, chips, and other goodies in reusable plastic containers instead of Baggies. Carry your drink in a Thermos bottle and your lunch in a lunch box.

5. Buy in bulk. Use empty coffee cans or other containers with lids to keep the products fresh.

6. Avoid buying products with excess packaging or with nonrecyclable packaging, such as plastic-and-paper bubble packs or drink boxes. When you see products with wasteful packaging, write a letter to the manufacturer. Most packages

have the address printed somewhere on them. Get your friends to write, too.

7. Look for the recycling symbol on packages and choose the brand that uses recycled packaging and content. You can even buy recycled school paper.

8. Carry your own reusable bags to the grocery store so that you don't have to take plastic or brown paper bags that would only be thrown away. If you must take a bag from a store, choose one you know you will reuse.

9. If you receive a wrapped gift, remove the paper neatly and save it to reuse. Save greeting cards to cut the front picture off and reuse as a gift tag. Use the other portions as notepaper.

10. Instead of using paper towels to wipe up spills or clean surfaces, use washable cloth towels and rags. Dirty paper towels can't be recycled. However, if you have to use paper towels, use them more than once. Most of them are strong enough to dry and be reused a number of times.

11. When cleaning up after a meal, put leftover food in hard, reusable glass, ceramic, or plastic containers instead of in plastic bags. Save glass jars or deli containers for this purpose and keep them out of the waste stream. If you need to use plastic bags, wash and reuse them.

Trash just thrown out on the street—with no concern for what will happen to it—must become a thing of the past.

12. If you receive a magazine or other mailing in a polyethylene cover, write to the senders telling them that you would rather see their magazine come in plain brown paper or, better yet, without a protective wrapping at all.

13. If you receive a lot of catalogs and other unasked-for mailings that you don't need or even read, you can have your name taken off major mailing lists by writing to: Mail Preference Service, Direct Marketing Association, P.O. Box 3861, 11 West 42nd St., New York, NY 10163-3861.

14. On the subject of mail, if you receive something in a sturdy, clean envelope, just cross off the address side and reuse it, putting the new address and stamp on the clean side. The postal service will pay attention to the new side.

15. Buy a battery recharger and rechargeable batteries. Rechargeable batteries cost more, but you will save ten or twenty times the original cost. Prolong the life of any battery by using a cord for the radio or other appliance when you are in reach of an electrical outlet.

16. Return reusable items whenever possible. For example, take steel hangers back to the dry cleaners and plastic flowerpots to the greenhouse.

17. Learn, and encourage your parents to learn, how to repair damaged appliances. Help them figure out how to get a lamp, toaster, or iron working again instead of throwing it away. There are many "how-to" books available to help you. Be sure to get help from an experienced person, however, before dealing with electricity.

18. Remember that water, too, has to be recycled. Avoid wasting it. Don't throw polluting liquids down the drain.

19. Consider the reusability of every item before you discard it or send it for recycling.

Beyond Your Home

Any place you go—school, church, club, business—can become a place where you can get recycling activities started and get other people caring about the Earth.

1. Tell others what you've learned about recycling and volunteer to help them recycle their waste.

2. Encourage your organizations to get involved in recycling projects. You could find a market for special items such as paint, appliances, or batteries. Plan a community collection day for the special items. Check with a university extension office or local environmental affairs office to find out about other organizations' programs.

3. Read Chapter 8 and learn all you can about your community's waste handling and plans for the future. If you develop an opinion about your community's plans or cur-

You can put your own caring for the environment to work by organizing groups to clean up after public events, making sure that recyclables are separated.

rent programs, express your opinion in writing to the appropriate people. Be sure you have valid reasons for your opinions and try to express them clearly. See the section below on writing letters for some ideas.

4. Find out whether your school, organizations, parents' businesses, and community offices use recycled materials whenever possible. If they don't, encourage them to begin. Study environmental magazines to get addresses of recycled paper and other suppliers.

5. Join environmental organizations. Such groups are listened to on a national and international basis. By joining, you are saying that you agree with their work on behalf of the environment. Contact the following:

Alliance to Save Energy, 1725 K St., NW, Washington, DC 20006

American Forestry Assn, 1516 P St., NW, Washington, DC 20036

Canadian Wildlife Federation, 1673 Carling Ave., Ottawa, Ontario, Canada K2A 3Z1

Environmental Defense Fund, 1616 P St., NW, Washington, DC 20036

Greenpeace USA, 1436 U St., NW, Washington, DC 20009

National Audubon Society, 801 Pennsylvania Ave., SE, Washington, DC 20003

National Wildlife Federation, 1400 16th St., NW, Washington, DC 20036

World Wildlife Fund, 1250 24th St., NW, Washington, DC 20037, or 60 St. Clair Ave., E., Suite 201, Toronto, Ontario, Canada M4T IN5

Writing Letters

You have opinions on what should happen to the world you will live in for the rest of your life. However, having an opinion does not do any good unless you make it known to the people who make policy. Let your legislators know what you think.

In writing a letter in which you express your opinion on controversial issues, follow these seven tips:

1. Make your letter one page or less. Cover only one subject in each letter.

2. Introduce yourself and tell why you, personally, are for or against the issue.

3. Be clear and to the point.

4. Be specific on whether you want the person to vote "yes" or "no."

5. Write as an individual. The environmental group you belong to will have already let the legislator know its stand on the issue.

6. When you get a response, write a follow-up letter to re-emphasize your position and give your reaction to your legislator's comments.

7. Write again to thank your legislators if they vote the way you asked them to.

State Concerns. On issues concerning state legislation or to express your opinion about actions taken by your state environmental or natural resources agency, you can write to:

Your local state legislator. Check at your local library to discover his or her name.

The governor of your state. Write in care of your state capital.

The director of your state's department of natural resources or related environmental agency. Check your local library for the specific person and the address.

Federal Concerns. On issues concerning federal legislation or to express your opinion about actions taken by the federal government, you can write to:

Your two state senators. Check at your local library to discover their names. Write:

> The Honorable _____
> U.S. Senate
> Washington, D.C. 20510

Your local congressman. Check at your local library to discover his or her name.

> The Honorable _____
> U.S. House of Representatives
> Washington, D.C. 20515

The President of the United States. He has the power to veto, or turn down, bills approved by the Senate and the House of Representatives. He also has final control over what the United States Environmental Protection Agency and other agencies do.

> President _____
> The White House
> 1600 Pennsylvania Avenue, N.W.
> Washington, D.C. 20501

A Final Reminder— Recycling . . .

1. Saves nonrenewable natural resources.

2. Saves energy, which is produced by fossil fuels. Burning fossil fuels emit chemicals that produce acid rain and contribute to global warming.

3. Keeps waste out of landfills.

4. Keeps toxins out of the incinerators.

5. Saves imports of oil, reducing the federal balance of payments.

6. Saves air and water from pollution.

7. Reduces the cost of getting rid of trash.

8. Keeps trees, needed to fight air pollution, from being cut down.

9. Helps to rescue our Earth for future generations.

REDUCE, REUSE, RECYCLE, and COMPOST!

IF YOU DON'T,

in the words of the Environmental Defense Fund,

YOU'RE THROWING IT ALL AWAY!

GLOSSARY

acid rain – precipitation that contains acids formed by the chemical reaction between water vapor and sulfur dioxide, nitrogen oxide, or other chemicals, generally from industrial pollutants.

aseptic box – a small box, usually used for beverages, that is made from multiple layers of materials and adhesives, making it nonrecyclable except as a mixed material.

biodegradable – able to break down through natural processes. Often used to refer to plastic that has a natural polymer, such as cornstarch or vegetable oil, added to it so that it breaks into smaller pieces when exposed to the right environment.

"bottle bill" – popular term for a law that requires all glass, aluminum, and plastic drink bottles to be returned for recycling.

chlorofluorocarbons (CFCs) – complex chemical combinations containing the elements carbon, chlorine, and fluorine. Because they do not combine easily with other substances, they are used to propel other chemicals out of spray cans and, as a gas, to make polystyrene plastic expand into a foam. Because they vaporize at low temperatures, they are used as cooling agents in refrigerators and air conditioners. They are also useful as cleaning chemicals.

composting – a process that speeds up the natural breakdown of organic material such as leaves, grass clippings, and food waste. It decays into a nutrient-rich material called humus that can be used as a fertilizer.

consumer – one who uses, or consumes, materials.

cullet – crushed glass that is melted down to make new glass.

dioxins – chemicals given off in the manufacturing or incineration of some plastics.

EPA – see **United States Environmental Protection Agency**

garbologist– a garbage scientist, who studies the things people throw away and what happens to them in landfills.

greenhouse effect – the accumulation of certain gases, such as carbon dioxide, in the atmosphere, where they trap the sun's heat, causing the average temperature around the earth gradually to rise.

groundwater – water beneath the earth's surface but above the underlying rock. In low-lying places it forms lakes and ponds. In high locations it is reached only by wells.

incineration – the deliberate burning of waste materials. When the heat given off is used to make steam to turn electrical generation turbines, the burning is called *waste-to-energy incineration.*

landfill – see **sanitary landfill.**

leachate – liquid (usually rain or snow melt) that passes through piled-up waste, becoming polluted. Leachate can pollute groundwater under a landfill.

methane – a colorless, odorless, flammable gas that is given off when garbage breaks down in landfills and dumps. It is also a major part of natural gas.

Materials Recovery Facility (MRF) – a place at which municipal waste, especially unsorted recyclables, is sorted into different materials in order to recycle as many as possible.

municipal – under the control of or deriving from a local government. Municipal waste is nonindustrial waste from residences and businesses.

nonrenewable – unable to be made again. Most natural resources, because they were formed within the Earth over millions of years, are nonrenewable.

photodegradable – able to be broken down by exposure to sunlight. Photodegradable plastics can not decompose in landfills because the sun cannot reach them.

polymer – a chemical made of large molecules linked together in long chains. Rubber is a natural polymer. Plastics are synthetic, or man-made, polymers.

precycling – reducing the amount of trash that you produce by choosing not to purchase or use certain wasteful items.

renewable – able to be grown or made again. When speaking of natural resources, living things such as trees are the only renewable ones.

resource recovery – another name for recycling that emphasizes the recovery and reuse of natural resources.

sanitary landfill – a site designated for the burial of wastes that is constructed so as to keep pollutants out of water and air. The waste is spread out, compacted, and covered with dirt.

sludge – sediment, or solid material that falls to the bottom of sewage tanks in waste-water treatment plants.

solid waste – all garbage, trash, and sludge and other wastes from any source except sewage from homes and business; especially, municipal solid waste (MSW).

sustainable – able to supply society's current needs without jeopardizing the ability to meet future needs. Sustainable development of natural resources is a goal of environmentalists.

thermoplastic – a type of plastic that becomes soft when it is heated or pressure is applied, and then hardens as it cools.

thermosetting – a type of durable plastic that cannot be softened by heat or pressure .

tire-derived fuel (TDF) – chopped-up tires which are incinerated at very high temperatures (2300°) to produce energy.

United States Environmental Protection Agency (EPA) – A federal government agency whose job it is to regulate factors of the environment and those that may be affecting it.

waste stream – the entire collection of waste from all sources, which must be dealt with in some way. Recycling keeps many materials out of the waste stream.

white goods – major household appliances, such as refrigerators, washing machines, stoves, and the like.

white paper – high-quality paper such as from offices. It is generally more valuable than most other types of paper for recycling.

INDEX

Bold number = illustration

R

railroad ties 33, 48
Rathje, William 22, 24
recyclables **66**, 96, **117**
recyclers 69, 72
RecycleSaurous **101**
recycling centers **35**, 71, 98
recycling, official 35
"Recycling Pete" **102**
recycling symbol 32, 37,
    55, **71**, 75, **77**, **81**,
    102, **103**, 115
reducing waste 9, 15, 29
refrigerators 85
renewable resources 17, 123
repairing 34
resins 77
resource recovery 34, 123
retreading tires **88**
reusing products 9, 15, **33**
Rhode Island 36
rubber 87, 88
rugs 91

S

Salvation Army 34, **62**
sandals 88
sanitary landfill, see landfill
Scandinavia 14
scrap 67, 68, 86, 98
senators 120
separation process 70
septic systems 52
sewage system 46, 52
sewers 14
silver 92
six-pack rings **79**
sludge 52, 123
soda ash 82
soil 45, 46, 52, 88, 93
solar system 39
solid waste, see waste
solid waste stream 78, 123
sorting recyclables 66
source separation 36
Soviet Union 71

"Spaceship Earth" 9
squeeze bottle 75
state government 100
Staten Island 19, 20
steel 36, **66-69**, 85, **86**,
    89, 98, 109
"Styro-Cop" 33
Styrofoam, see polystyrene
    foam
sulfates 42
sulfur 16, 41, 42
sulfur dioxide 42
sulfuric acid 42
synthetic rubber 87

T

taxes 96, 101
TDF 89, 123
telephone books 24
Texas 7
textiles 33, 47, 57, **91**
Thames, River 53
thermoplastic 74, 123
thermosetting 74, 123
3RC 16, 29, 113, 114
throwaway products, see
    disposables
"Throwaway" Society 13
timber industry 56
tin cans 67
tipping floor 65
tire dumps 87, 89
tire-derived fuel **84**, 89,
    123
tires **34**, 84, **86-89**
town dump **12**, 100
toxins 121
trash, see waste
trash as natural resource 27
trash collection, in China 20
trash collection, in Egypt 20
trash-collection trucks **15**,
    19, **36**, **43**, 65, 95, 100
trees 17, 27, 57,
    60, 106, 110, 121
trucks, see trash-collection
    trucks

U-V

U.S. federal government 56
U.S. Forest Service 56
ultraviolet light 75
United Nations 103
United States 12, 13, 14, 22,
    53, 62, 74, 87, 88, 90,
    93, 102
United States Environmental
    Protection Agency 65,100
University of Arizona 22
University of Wisconsin 33
Vermont 98
Virginia 87, **99**

W

wallboard 60
Washington State 36, 93
waste 7, 8, 11, 14, **23**,
    98, 107, 113
waste analysis 22, **23**, **99**
waste as fuel 16
waste stream 68, 96
waste-to-energy 16, **17**
wasteful packaging, see excess
    packaging
water 39, 93, 116
water cycle 50, 51
water pollution 15,**51**,53, 60
wells, monitoring 19
white goods 85, 123
white paper **60**, 123
windrows 47
Wisconsin 33, **95**, 98
wood fiber 56, 57, 60
wood-pulp fluff 106
World War II **62**, 66
World Wildlife Fund 118
writing letters 115,
    116, 118-120

Y-Z

yard waste 14, 43-49, 101
zabbaleens 20
zinc 87, 92

PHOTO SOURCES

ABOUT THE AUTHORS

Jean F. Blashfield and Wallace B. Black are dedicated environmentalists, writers, and publishers who are responsible for this book and the SAVING PLANET EARTH series. Working together, with other environmentalists, educators, and Childrens Press, they have developed 13 other books in the SAVING PLANET EARTH series.

This creative team was responsible for the creation of THE YOUNG PEOPLE'S SCIENCE ENCYCLOPEDIA and ABOVE AND BEYOND, THE ENCYCLOPEDIA OF AVIATION AND SPACE SCIENCES. In addition, Jean Blashfield was the editor-in-chief of THE YOUNG STUDENTS ENCYCLOPEDIA and is author of more than 20 other books. Wallace Black, a former pilot in the United States Air Force, is the author of a series of books on World War II.